venerable
mahā sthavira sangharakshita

THE PATH
OF THE INNER LIFE

FWBO Publications
London
1975

The Path of The Inner Life
published by The Friends of The Western Buddhist Order
1a, Balmore Street, London, N.19.

First Edition: April 1975

Copyright F.W.B.O. London 1975

Printed by F.W.B.O. Printing Service
3, Plough Lane, Purley, Surrey, England.

contents

introduction

To give any experience a definition is to clothe it irrevocably in the cloak of mortality. I can think of nothing to which this applies more than the area of spiritual or religious experience. The insights and aspirations which all of us have in our moments of vision are, of all human experiences, most subject to this most tyrannical of rulers, impermanence. The whole field of spiritual development is a labyrinth peopled with ghosts and fraught with distractions, in the coils of which many eminent travellers have perished. To attempt to write about such a field is, at any time, a difficult undertaking, and one which is made more arduous today, as well as much more urgently necessary, by the many different systems and organisations which exist side by side, and express their views on the matter with considerable force.

It is therefore with heartfelt admiration and an ever increasing sense of wonder that I have read the following essays, some of them several times, and each reading has made me more conscious of what to me are their most satisfying qualities: their total sincerity and complete lack of dogmatism. To my mind these are the qualities which make the difference between mere expression and true literature, and they are becoming increasingly difficult to find in present day writing; yet, in a field such as that with which this book is concerned, they are essential to the success of the endeavour. At a time when opinions on just about any subject can be had for the price of a Sunday newspaper, to come across deep experience of life sincerely communicated in a style which is at once universal and immediately personal is like finding a diamond in the

4

midst of a heap of ashes.

To read these essays is to re-create for oneself all the strivings and idealisms of past civilisations, and to live again through the eyes and minds of those who have most contributed to human thought. Sangharakshita is as at home in the worlds of Socrates and Homer as he is in those of Spencer and Hume, and he is able to bring together their manifold viewpoints on existence with a warmth and lucidity which is welcome in the often dark chambers of intellectual thought. And in the end all philosophies and existential viewpoints are transfigured by the all-embracing vision of Buddhism so eloquently and poetically set forth in these pages.

I can do no more here than wish the reader a stimulating and fruitful journey through some of the most meaningful and magical domains of thought known to Man.

September 1974   ANANDA

preface

Most of the essays in this volume were written in the years
1949 and 1950, and while most of them made their first
appearance in the pages of *The Aryan Path* (Bombay), others
came out in *The Middle Way* (London), *The Maha Bodhi
Journal* (Calcutta), and *The Buddhist* (Colombo). To the editors
of these journals I am grateful for permission to reprint.

The essays were therefore written fairly early in life, when
I was in my mid-twenties. At least two were written in Benares,
during the period which I spent there with Ven. Jagdish Kashyap,
my teacher in Pali, Abhidhamma and Logic; one was composed
in Rajgir, in the course of a pilgrimage which I made with Ven.
Kashyap to 'The Land of the Great Disciples'; and the remainder
saw the light of day in Kalimpong, which means that they
belong to the same period of literary activity as the editorial
articles contributed to *Stepping-Stones* and subsequently col-
lected in *Crossing the Stream.*

Looking back on those days, and re-reading these essays
after nearly a quarter of a century, one naturally sees a somewhat different 'self' and a somewhat different mode of
expression. Yet, though I now see certain things more clearly
than I did then, and though I would not now write in quite
the style of those days, there is nothing of importance in these
writings with which I disagree, and nothing—except for an
occasional looseness of terminology—which I would wish to
correct. Indeed, there are a number of passages which express
basic convictions—even basic insights—with a force and clarity
on which, after twenty-four or twenty-five years, I find myself
unable to improve. I therefore send these essays out again into

the world, in their new garb, in the hope that, under the transcendental influence of all the Buddhas and Bodhisattvas, they may be a means of helping at least a few more people find, and tread, the Path of the Inner Life.

SANGHARAKSHITA

Tittleshall,
NORFOLK.

December 12th 1973

THE PATH OF THE INNER LIFE

Religion is not a matter for blind belief or intellectual assent, but for living faith and energetic practice. It consists not in the acceptance of any creed or dogma but in the achievement of an experience, or rather in the achievement of a number of experiences. These experiences link up into a series. This continuous series of experiences forms a Path or Way. When we consider it with regard to its direction it appears as an inward-going as opposed to an outward-going Way, as a Path of the Inner rather than of the Outer Life. Since it is a matter of immediate personal experience within the heart-depths of the individual devotee, and since such experience is by its very nature incommunicable, it is spoken of as an Esoteric as opposed to an Exoteric Path, as a Doctrine of the Heart rather than as a Doctrine of the Eye. When we realize that those experiences are not simply aggregated round any unchanging ego-entity or permanent core of separative self-hood, but that they are, on the contrary, processes of progressive self-impoverishment, self-annihilation, the Path appears as a Way of Emptiness; but, since the "seeming void" is in reality "full", it also appears as a Way of Compassion. Finally, when we regard it as a Path which runs not only between but also above all mind-made dualities, it is seen as a Middle Way.

When speaking of the Path of the Inner Life we automatically contra-distinguish it from the Path of the Outer Life. The distinction consists not so much in a difference of position as in a difference of direction. That is to say, it is to be understood not statically but dynamically. The Path of the Inner Life is also known as the *Nirvritti Marga* or inward-circling

8

path and that of the Outer Life as the *Pravritti Marga* or out-ward-circling path. That which "circles" either inwards or outwards is the mind. The natural tendency of the mind is to spread itself out fan-wise, as it were, over the five objects of the senses. This outward-circling or fan-wise-spreading move-ment of the average human mind is naturally accompanied by a corresponding disturbance of the psychic harmony of the subject and a diminution of the sum total of his psychic energy. Just as the brilliance of a beam of light diminishes as it is spread out over a wider and wider area, so the power of the mind decreases as it is scattered over a larger and larger number of objects. The more concentrated the mind becomes, the more powerful it grows and the more deeply it is able to penetrate into the fathomless abyss of Truth. The mind which is engrossed in the pleasures of the five senses is unconcentrated and therefore impotent. It is unable to see things as they really are. The Buddha and His enlightened disciples of all ages and climes proclaim as though with one voice that *Prajna* or transcendental wisdom arises only in the concentrated mind, and that the mind becomes concentrated only when it is purified of all taint of earthly desires.

The first step along the Path of the Inner Life, without which no other step can be taken, is to become "indifferent to objects of perception." Such indifference is never the result of satiety, but is, on the contrary, the slowly-ripening fruit of constant perseverance in stern renunciation. "Do not believe that lust can ever be killed out if gratified or satiated, for this is an abomination inspired by Mara," warns *The Voice of Silence.* The early stages of the career of a spiritual aspirant are a period of unceasing struggle between the lower and higher impulses of his nature. On the outcome of this struggle depends the success or failure of his vocation. If he is able to resist the solicitations of the objects of perception and turn his senses as it were inside out, like the five fingers of a glove, thus reversing their direction, they will merge into a single inner sense, and with this subtle inner sense he will be able to perceive spiritual realities. Mystical religion has therefore ever stressed, as indispensable preliminaries to any attempt to know the Truth that will make us free, the killing out of all desire for sense-pleasures and the withdrawal of the scattered forces of the mind into a single unified focus of attention. Only by becoming deaf and blind to the outward illusion can we develop that subtle "inner touch" that will enable us to intuit the Truth that sounds and shines within.

But this purely spiritual perception of spiritual realities by the inner spiritual sense differs from that of our other states of consciousness, inasmuch as it does not take place within the framework of the subject-object relation. The chasm which ordinarily yawns between the experient subject and the object of his experience becomes more and more narrow until finally it disappears and he knows the Truth by becoming one with it. Therefore it is written: "Thou canst not travel on the Path before thou hast become that Path itself." In the vigorous words of the Buddha, we have to "make the path become." This path-becoming is therefore also a self-becoming, a process of self-development, self-transformation, self-realization. The Goal of the Path, the Ultimate Experience in which the whole long series of experiences eventually culminates, is the state designated as Nirvana.

Since the Path of the Inner Life consists essentially in a series of experiences, and since all experiences are by their very nature ineffable, it is also an Esoteric as opposed to an Exoteric Path. Nothing in the religious life is truly esoteric save spiritual experience. The most private ritual, the abstrusest philosophical doctrine, the most jealously guarded scripture, the most secret society or organization, are all exoteric. They belong to the domain of "Head-learning" rather than to the domain of "Soul-wisdom" and, as *The Voice of the Silence* emphatically admonishes us, it is above all things necessary to learn to separate the one from the other, to learn to discriminate between "The Doctrine of the Eye" and "The Doctrine of the Heart".

Many, unfortunately, think that the secret teaching consists of some piece of information about the evolution of the universe or the constitution of man which has not been communicated to the world at large, and that it is necessary to acquire this information from certain mysterious personages supposed to be hiding themselves in inaccessible corners of the earth. Such "secret teachings" or, for the matter of that, whole libraries of secret scriptures and orders of secret teachers, may indeed exist, but they all belong to the Exoteric Path, to the domain of Head-learning, and are of little value in the spiritual life. Indeed, they are often in the highest degree harmful to it, for those who believe that they have learned the "esoteric doctrine" and become "initiates" generally grow so proud of their fancied superiority to the rest of mankind that for them progress along the true Esoteric Path is barred for a long time to come. That is why *The Voice of the Silence* is "Dedicated to the Few." The *Hridaya Dharma* or Heart-Doctrine which was transmitted by the Lord Buddha to His immediate disciples, and which was handed on by them to their disciples and their disciples' disciples, even down to the present day, does not consist of any formulated doctrine, much less still any written scripture, but was simply His own ineffable experience of Nirvana. The true Esoteric Path, the true Secret Teaching, the true Doctrine of the Heart, the true Master, is not to be found in any book, or, indeed, anywhere at all in the outside world, but in the heart-depths of the spiritual experience of the individual devotee.

Although the Path of Inner Life, the Esoteric Path, consists of a series of experiences eventually culminating in the Supreme Experience designated Nirvana, these experiences are not "acquisitions" of the subject in the sense that material things and even learning are acquisitions. The one root-illusion which prevents us from seeing things as they really are, and which

11

it is the primary business of spiritual practice to remove, is the belief in ourselves as separate, perduring individual selves or ego-entities. Inseparably linked with this belief is the feeling of possession, the desire for acquisition. The concepts of "I" and "mine" are simply the two sides of a single coin. As, therefore, the aspirant progresses along the Path of the Inner Life or, better still, as he more and more becomes that Path, the false sense of separative selfhood, the feeling of possession and the greed for acquisition are simultaneously attenuated and eventually disappear together. The further, therefore, the aspirant progresses along the Path, or the more truly he becomes it, the harder it is for him to dichotomize his experience into a subject and an object and to speak of the latter as though it was a possession or acquisition of the former. In the Supreme Experience of Nirvana such a claim would have become a complete impossibility. The Buddha therefore declared that those who laid claim to any spiritual attainment as though they had made it their personal property thereby only betrayed the hollowness of their pretensions.

The decisive test of whether any experience is truly spiritual or not consists in ascertaining whether it is possible to speak of it as "my" experience or not. If it is possible truthfully to speak of it in this way it is simply an addition to the mental or emotional furniture of the ego and as such is merely mundane. This is the meaning of the choice which the aspirant is called upon to make between the "Open Path", the Path of the pseudo-Arahant, and the "Secret Path", the Path of the Bodhisattva. The Arahant is popularly supposed to be one who is indifferent to the miseries of sentient beings and therefore does not remain on earth to help them but disappears into the private bliss of a purely individual Nirvana; whereas the Bodhisattva is supposed to be one whose heart is so profoundly moved by the woes of the world that he decides to renounce the "sweet but selfish rest" of Nirvana and to devote himself to the alleviation of human misery even to the end of time.

12

The choice which the aspirant has to make between these two Paths constitutes his severest test and final initiation.

Although the popular doctrine represents both the Open Path and the Secret Path as genuine alternatives, the Way to Nirvana is in fact only one. The Path of pseudo-Arahantship, of individual liberation, in fact represents the temptation to think of the Supreme Experience as something which can be possessed privately by the individual subject. The renunciation of the thought that Nirvana is something to be attained is the last condition precedent for the "attainment" of Nirvana. Where there is the feeling of possession, of "my-ness", there is also the sense of separative selfhood, of "I-ness", and so long as this sense of separative selfhood persists, liberation is impossible, for liberation is fundamentally nothing but liberation from this same root-illusion of separative selfhood. Neither Arahantship nor Bodhisattvahood, which are simply the same realization in predominantly intellectual and predominantly emotional perspectives, can be attained without the complete renunciation of the ideas of "I" and "mine".

The Path of the Inner Life is spoken of as a Way of Emptiness because it consists in the progressive attenuation of the ego-sense, and the gradual intensification of the realization that everything is devoid of separative selfhood, that all is intrinsically pure and void. This void is not, however, a zero or nothingness. Buddhists express this truth by saying that the Void is itself void. Just as the "seeming full" is void, so also the "seeming void" is full. This fullness or rather overflowingness of the seeming void is what we call Compassion. Since Compassion is not an inert principle or a static somewhat but a purely transcendental activity, it is frequently personified as Amitabha Buddha, Avalokiteshwara, Kwan Yin etc. In the magnificent but still inadequate words of *The Voice of the Silence*,

Compassion is no attribute. It is the Law of LAWS— eternal Harmony, Alaya's SELF; a shoreless universal essence, the light of everlasting right, and fitness of all things, the law of Love eternal.

The more attenuated the ego-sense becomes, the more abundantly will selfless activities be manifested, for the Way of Emptiness is also the Way of Compassion, and to become one therefore means to become the other also. Emptiness and Compassion, Wisdom and Love, are the static and dynamic aspects, respectively, of the one Supreme State of Nirvana. The Arahant ideal stresses the former, the Bodhisattva ideal the latter; but the goal is the same for both, and the eradication of the ego-sense is indispensably necessary in either path. Self-enlightenment and compassionate activity for the sake of all sentient beings are mutually exclusive alternatives only on the level of the dichotomizing intellect. In reality they are the intension and extension, the depth and the breadth, of a single realization which is at once both emptiness and compassion.

The Arahant-ideal is unattainable by him who imagines that he has an individual self which is in bondage and which must be liberated: the self *is* the bondage. The Bodhisattva-ideal is unattainable by him who imagines that there are separate individual beings for him to save.

Buddha said: "Subhuti, all the Bodhisattva-Heroes should discipline their thoughts as follows: all living creatures . . . are caused by Me to attain Unbounded Liberation, Nirvana. Yet when vast, uncountable, immeasurable numbers of beings have thus been liberated, verily no being has been liberated. Why is this, Subhuti? It is because no Bodhisattva who is a real Bodhisattva cherishes the idea of an ego-entity, a personality, a being, or a separated individuality."*

Emptiness and Activity, *Prajna* and *Karuna*, Wisdom and Compassion, are in reality not two but one, which is ineffable Nirvana, and the paths which lead thereto, the Path of the Arahant, and the Path of the Bodhisattva, are also one, which is the One Way (*Ekayana*), the Way of the Buddha (*Buddha-*

*The Jewel of Transcendental Wisdom, p.26.

14

yana).

Finally, since the Path of the Inner Life avoids such extremes as those of self-indulgence and self-torture, Nihilism and Eternalism, self-reliance and other-reliance, individualism and altruism, together with the mutually exclusive deformations of the "Arahant" and "Bodhisattva" ideals, it is spoken of as the *Majjhima Patipada* or Middle Way. It should not, however, be supposed that as such it is simply a compromise between two antagonistic positions or an effort to solve antinomies on the same level of experience at which they arise. The Middle Way lies not so much between extremes as above them. It is not the lowest common denominator of two contradictory terms but the Higher Third wherein both find perfect mutual solution. The numberless antinomies which arise on the ordinary levels of human experience can be resolved only by attaining to a relatively higher level of experience. Intellectual problems are finally solved only by spiritual realization. To follow the Middle Path means to cultivate the practice of solving the conflicts of life and the contradictions of experience by rising above the level at which they are possible. The Middle Way is therefore essentially a Way of Spiritual Experience, and as such coincides with the Path of the Inner Life. Since all such conflicts and contradictions are products of the ego-sense, and can be solved only by rising above it, it also coincides with the Way of Emptiness, and therefore with the Way of Compassion too.

When we see that the Path of the Inner Life, the true Esoteric Path, the Way of Emptiness and the Way of Compassion and the Middle Way, are all aspects of the One Way, the Way taught by the Buddha, we begin to glimpse the profound truth of the saying that "The Path is one for all, the means to reach the goal must vary with the Pilgrims."

15

RELIGION AS REVELATION
AND AS DISCOVERY

The study of the Science of Comparative Religion, inaugurated in Asia by the Buddha (*Digha Nikaya, Brahmajala Sutta*) and in Europe by Roger Bacon (*Opus Majus*), is one of the most fascinating subjects to which the mind of man can possibly devote itself. The spectacle of the millennia-long struggle of humanity towards the Truth cannot fail to arouse the deepest and most poignant emotions in the breast of him who contemplates it with genuine interest and sympathy. For the history of Religion is, in fact, the history of man; not, indeed, of the peripheral and accidental man, but of the central and essential man; not of his physical body and material environment, but of that profoundest and most pregnant part of him which we may call his mind or heart (Indian *citta*, Chinese *hsin*). It is not the history of the memorable deeds he has done, of the great empires he has founded, of the immense wealth he has wrung from the bosom of nature, but of the character which he has formed, of the degree of inner illumination which he has attained, or of what, in a word, he has become.

The totem and fetish of the savage, to say nothing of the religious doctrines and philosophical systems of his civilized descendants, awaken in us vague feelings of sympathy which is almost reminiscence. For we are all bound on the same pilgrimage, have passed through the same stages of development, and therefore hold in the present moment of our consciousness the accumulated inheritance of all that man has ever thought and felt and done. We have sacrificed our children to Moloch, we have severed the sacred mistletoe with a sickle of gold, we have danced in drunken frenzy on the moonlit hills of Thrace;

and we, too, perhaps, have listened enraptured to the Sermon on the Mount, or heard some Buddha, Bodhisattva or Arahant unfolding before us the mysteries of the Good Law. The samskaras or active impressions created by those experiences still live within us and vibrate whenever the simulacrum of the object which originally imprinted them appears.

The study of the Science of Comparative Religion is therefore in truth the study of the evolution of our own consciousness. Herein lies the secret of its tremendous fascination. Moreover, it enables us, when properly studied, to see the various grades and species of religious experience not as isolated or unconnected events in man's mental life, but as the intimately interrelated component parts of a great pyramid of consciousness the apex whereof is the Consummation of Incomparable Enlightenment (*Anuttara Samyak Sambodhi*).

But the researches and investigations which a host of anthropologists, archaeologists, philologists, and historians have been making for more than a century have placed before the student of Comparative Religion such a bewilderingly rich variety of material in such astounding quantities that he is now in grave danger of being unable to see the wood for the trees. It has thus become imperatively necessary to divide religions into types and classes in order to transform the chaos of mere unrelated facts into the cosmos of an exact science. We are familiar with such divisions as natural and revealed; true and false; natural, anthropological and psychological; of finite mind, infinite mind and absolute mind; theistic, atheistic, pantheistic and so on. Others more elaborate and strictly scientific have also been suggested. But that division of religions which we are about to consider is not only perhaps more fundamental than any of these but moreover of vital importance in the dharmic or normative life.

The problem of whether Religion is essentially a revelation of truth *to* man or a discovery of truth *by* man is in fact the intellectual formulation of a spiritual difficulty which

17

each one of us experiences in the course of his or her quest for Reality. The most obvious and natural grouping of the various religions and sects of the world is, therefore, into those for whom Religion consists in revelation, and those for whom it consists of discovery, of the Truth. This division is not simply theoretical, since each of these definitions of Religion has exercized a profoundly modifying influence upon the entire body of the beliefs and practices of the religions which were, whether consciously or unconsciously, dominated by it. Perhaps it was with the thought of some such division in his mind that Stanislas Schayer wrote of Buddhism as "the most profound and most fundamental antithesis to Christianity".* Nor is this division wholly new. Far-Eastern Buddhists have long been familiar with the classification of religions into those depending on 'self-power', in Japanese *jiriki*, and those depending on 'other-power', or *tariki*. And in India religious aspirants are sometimes spoken of as displaying the characteristics of the young monkey, which clings fast to the hair of its mother's belly, and of the kitten, which is simply carried about helpless in her mouth.

Religion-as-Revelation holds that the existence of Religion in the world, and therefore the possibility of the attainment of Salvation or Emancipation by man, is ultimately dependent on the Object, the Other, and that the initiative in the matter belongs wholly to It or Him. It conceives the spiritual life not as the progressive actualization of a perfection potentially present in man but as the acceptance of something which he would never have been able to acquire by means of his own unaided efforts. Consequently, it tends to stress the weakness and sinfulness of human nature and to emphasize the necessity of extra-terrestrial intervention in the affairs of humanity. It is therefore only natural that Reality should be conceived as personal, and that the founders of the various

*The Religions of the World, The Ramakrishna Mission Institute of Culture, Calcutta, 1938, Vol.I, page 218.

religions and sects should be regarded as prophets or messengers (*nabi, rasul, messiah*) sent from, or as full or partial incarnations (*avatara*) of, Him. The written record of the message, teaching or life of each such founder is invariably regarded as the word of God Himself, and to doubt, question or criticize it is considered not only to preclude all possibility of salvation but even to run the risk of eternal damnation. Religion-as-Revelation therefore places the strongest possible emphasis on faith in God, faith in His prophet, messenger or incarnation, faith in His infallible Word, faith in His Church, faith in His priest. Unfortunately, the beliefs of the various founders, scriptures and churches which are included in this group of religions often disagree not only among themselves but also with those which are included in the other group. Hideous fanaticism and ferocious persecution thus ensue. Since each such religion regards its own particular revelation as the supreme and incontrovertible source of Truth the possibility of an appeal to reason and experience is automatically precluded. Obviously God would not wittingly contradict Himself. One revelation must therefore be true, and the remainder false, that is to say, not revelations at all but simply human fictions and inventions. Moreover, Religion-as-Revelation's house is divided not only against itself but against many other houses as well—against Science, for instance, which has succeeded in demonstrating the fallibility of many an infallible scripture. Is it, then, a matter for wonder that Religion-as-Revelation is fast losing its hold upon the hearts and minds of reflective men and women throughout the world?

Religion-as-Discovery, on the other hand, holds that Religion is essentially a manifestation of the human spirit, that man is able to discover the Way to Truth himself by means of his own unaided human efforts, that the attainment of liberating knowledge depends upon the subject or self, and that the initiative in the matter rests ultimately within the abysm of one's own volition. It would envisage the dharmic or normative life not as the engraftment of some exotic blossom onto the barren stock of humanity but as the flowering forth of its native perfection from the seed within. Consequently, it is inclined rather to inspire man by appealing to his innate strength and goodness than to discourage him by dwelling upon his mistakes and failures. Instead of imagining an arbitrary divine intervention to be the most important event in history it asserts the supremacy of natural law and maintains that the aspiration towards emancipation must, like every other process, proceed in accordance with an eternal and universal order (*sanatana dhamma*). It is therefore hardly surprizing that Religion-as-Discovery conceives Reality as a suprapersonal principle of knowledge or state of consciousness or that it regards the religious founder simply as one who, after himself realizing that principle or state, teaches humanity the way thereto. The records of his life and teachings are only a map describing the Way, a raft to cross the stream, or a finger pointing to the moon. They demand not blind faith but clear-sighted understanding, they appeal not to some infallible authority but to reason and experience. Religion-as-Discovery is therefore not only tolerant of all other religious beliefs and practices, howsoever divergent from its own, but is able to join hands with earnest seekers after truth in every sphere of human activity. It sees Science not as an enemy but as a friend and fellow worker.

The last two paragraphs have presented the two principal conceptions of Religion in what may be described as their 'chemically pure' state. But if we are to proceed in accordance with the spirit of the Science of Comparative Religion we shall not leave them in a position of uncomfortable antithesis but will try, instead, to discover the psychological basis of their divergence. This will not only enable us to understand their mutual relation but also to determine their respective positions in the hierarchy of consciousness.

Understanding is impossible without sympathy. Let us therefore project ourselves, as it were, into the mind of one who feels the necessity of revelation and try to understand his condition from within rather than from without. The two elements which play the chief roles in such a mind are an intense aspiration towards Reality and an overwhelming sense of its inability to attain thereto. A feeling of continual frustration therefore naturally ensues and in time becomes so intense that the subject is willing to adopt any available means of bringing to a speedy end the terrible stress and and tension by which he is tormented. It is therefore with a sense of tremendous relief that he casts the whole responsibility for his salvation upon the shoulders of the Other. He receives with joy and gratitude the gospel of salvation by simple faith and goes out in an ecstasy of adoration towards whoever proclaims that it is sufficient to trust in Him.

Upon extricating ourselves from the antinomy of such a consciousness we are naturally prompted to ask why it should have been unable to attain to Reality by means of its own unaided efforts. In order to answer this question we shall have to consider in what cultural and religious environment this antinomic consciousness most commonly arises.

The matter is not difficult to determine. The three extant Semitic religions, Judaism, Christianity and Islam, are clearly all dominated by the conception of Religion-as-Revelation. All believe in a self-revealing God, all possess an infallible sacred book, and all believe, albeit in different ways, in someone supposed to be sent to man from God. Let us also consider in what cultural and religious environment the opposite type of consciousness most commonly arises. Buddhism and Taoism are perhaps the only religions which consistently adhere, in their oldest and most authoritative scriptures, to the conception of Religion-as-Discovery. Hinduism as a whole wavers uncertainly between the two conceptions. The Yogadarshana, which is affiliated to Buddhism, inclines for instance toward one, while the two Mimamsas, which are weighed down by the burden of Vedic authority, and various devotional schools, which are theistic and incarnationist, incline toward the other.

Having thus determined which religions and sects conceive Religion as revelation, and which regard it as discovery, we are in a position to enquire whether there is present in the various systems belonging to each group any common factor which predisposes them to view Religion in the two ways described. Such a factor there indeed is. It is the presence in Buddhism of a graded path of Sila, Samadhi and Panna—a clear and comprehensive Way leading progressively from the lowest point of mundane to the loftiest pinnacle of supra-mundane consciousness and its absence in Judaism, Christianity and Islam, that is the principal cause of the difference between their respective conceptions of Religion. It is a startling but nevertheless completely verifiable fact that neither in the Old Testament of the Christians, nor yet in the Muslim Quran, is there anything even remotely approaching the scheme of systematic self-culture comprized in the Middle Way or Ariyan Eightfold Path of Buddhism. Christ has truly said that "The Kingdom of Heaven is within you"; but the Christian Scriptures contain only a few scattered and unconnected hints on how to realize it. The same may be said of Judaism and Islam.

It is, of course, true that each of these three great faiths produced a large number of spiritually gifted men and women who not only regarded Religion as discovery but even progressed along the Path themselves and described many of its stages for the benefit of their friends and followers. Such were the Kabbalists among the Jews, the Mystics among the Christians, and the Sufis among the Muslims. But these persons were not only regarded with the gravest suspicion, and even violently persecuted, by their more orthodox co-religionists, but are regarded by modern students of Comparative Religion as being subject to strong influences of Indian origin. Thus A.C. Bouqet, an Anglican clergyman, writes ". . . the pseudo-Dionysius [universally regarded as the

22

fountain-head of medieval Christian mysticism] is only super-
ficially Christian, and has a quite different religion as its real
basis . . . . Mysticism of the non-Christian type is perfectly
at home in the religious life of Indians. Hence those parallels
to the Christian mystics of the Middle Ages which have been
found in Hindu and Buddhist literature and to which attention
has been drawn, are not in the least surprizing, and do not
mean that the Christian mystics in question have an affinity
with the Hindus by virtue of their Christianity, but purely
in consequence of their having steeped themselves in a
particular apocryphal writing, which is based upon the writings
of the Levantine pagan mystic, Proclus."* Dean Inge, the
celebrated modern representative of Christian Neoplatonism,
has been branded, like Shankara in India, as "a disguised
Buddhist". Sufism developed largely in consequence of the
spiritualizing influence exercized by Buddhism and Vedanta
on primitive Islam. Even Taoism is not wholly free from the
suspicion of Buddhist influence. We moreover observe that
with the growth of mysticism, whether in its Jewish, Christian
or Muslim forms, there is a corresponding development of the
characteristics associated with the conception of Religion as
essentially a process of discovery and realization. The great
mystics are consequently disinclined to stress the infallibility
of any scripture, declaring instead that the light can shine
forth only from within; they display a rare tolerance and
breadth of vision which the fanaticism and narrowmindedness
surrounding them serve to make more conspicuous; they
proclaim with one voice that Religion is a Path to be followed,
a Realization to be won, not a ritual to be performed or a
creed to be believed.

Conversely, when certain Buddhist sects, such as that founded
by Nichiren, degenerated into Religion-as-Revelation, and began
to regard the Buddha as a self-revealing Deity, the Saddharma-
pundarika Sutra as His infallible revelation to mankind,

*Comparative Religion, New Edition, 1945, page 33.

23

and Nichiren himself as His inspired messenger, and, in a word, began to exhibit all the characteristics of the conception of Religion as essentially revelation, they naturally adopted an intolerant and hostile attitude towards all other sects. Needless to say, they laid more stress on faith in the Deity, the Scripture and the Prophet than in the cultivation of the threefold Path of Sila, Samadhi and Panna. Scarcely better is the attitude of certain pseudo-Theravadins who maintain that it is impossible to tread the Path or attain Nibbana in the present age, and that one should, therefore, simply fold his hands in resignation and await the advent of Metteyya Buddha. The careful student of Comparative Religion will be able to discover numerous examples of this highly significant correlation of the presence or absence of a progressive Path with the conception of Religion-as-Discovery and Religion-as-Revelation respectively.

We are now able to see that these two principal conceptions of Religion are not merely antithetical, but that one is comprehended by the other. The Middle Way or Ariyan Eightfold Path exists everywhere, for suffering exists everywhere; but it is not always perceived. Those who do not perceive it, together with those who have, having perceived a little of it and trodden it to that extent, naturally feel the need of revelation and tend to think of Religion as something that satisfies that need. Religion-as-Revelation is not opposed to, or unconnected with, Religion-as-Discovery, but is simply the product of a psychological difficulty which arises when one is either unable or unwilling to tread the Path to its end. Religion-as-Discovery just as a stage of the Path is included in the whole Path, and as our partial and fragmentary mundane consciousness is comprehended in the supra-mundane universal consciousness of Supreme Buddhahood.

THE 'PROBLEM' OF AHIMSA

The theoretical consideration of spiritual truths, without the actual practice of them in daily life, generally results in intellectual confusion. What was crystal-clear to the heart of the devotee becomes an insoluble problem in the eyes of the mere philosopher. Such has been the case with the great principle of *ahimsa*. It is torn out of the living context of actual practice and, after being applied to all sorts of imaginary situations and impossible exigencies of conduct, it is treated as a problem which calls for merely intellectual solution. One is asked whether he would use violence to protect the chastity of his mother or his sister, or whether he would feel himself justified in taking the life of one man in order to preserve the lives of a hundred men. It is furthermore pointed out that, since life is able to exist at all only by crowding the weaker forms of life out of existence, a completely non-violent life is a contradiction in terms, and the doctrine of *ahimsa* consequently an impossible ideal, a mere counsel of perfection, which cannot be realized at all in this violent world, and the logical consequence of which is, or would be if life followed logic, simply suicide. Having thus thoroughly confused his own mind and the minds of those who were foolish enough to listen to him, the armchair-philosopher triumphantly concludes that it is quite useless even to try to practise *ahimsa* and that one had better let the world go on in the same bad old way that it did before one was born and will go on, presumably, after one is dead.

The first thing that we shall have to do before we can clean up this intellectual mess is to decide in what *himsa* and *ahimsa* really consist. The Buddha has made it clear that the criterion by which the ethical status of an action is to be determined is the purity or impurity of the state of mind by which it was inspired. The mind is said to be pure when it is free from desire (*lobha*), hatred (*dosa*) and ignorance (*moha*) and impure when it is not free from these three defiling tendencies. An action is ethical or unethical not because it conforms to or does not conform to a predetermined scheme of do's and don't's but because it is rooted in states of mind which make for liberation or which make for bondage. *Himsa* and *ahimsa* are therefore primarily states of consciousness in which love (*adosa*) and hatred (*dosa*) respectively predominate. We shall see later on, however, that although they are essentially attitudes of mind rather than specific actions they nevertheless tend to express themselves outwardly in the field of life and action in a determinate manner.

Since *ahimsa* is fundamentally a condition of heart or a state of consciousness, the practice of *ahimsa* must consist primarily in the cultivation of that condition or state. It does not consist in the observance of any number however large, of rules, nor in the observance of any system of precautions, however elaborate, against even the accidental taking of life. What we may designate as the legalistic view of *ahimsa* is an attempt to solve the "problem" of non-violent action purely on the intellectual plane; it does not succeed in rising to the level of spiritual perception. It tends to make the practice of *ahimsa* a mechanical observance rather than a flaming passion. *In the sphere of ethics to try to determine what one should do before one has found out what to think and how to feel is a case of "putting the cart before the horse".*

The particular defiling tendency of mind to which violence (*himsa*) is affiliated is, as we have already seen, hatred (*dosa*). The practice of *ahimsa* therefore consists in the eradication of hatred (*dosa*) and the cultivation of love (*adosa*). But since hatred (*dosa*) is, like desire (*lobha*), in turn affiliated to

26

ignorance (*moha*), the practice of *ahimsa* consists, in the last analysis, in the eradication of ignorance (*moha*) and the cultivation of wisdom (*prajna, bodhi*). *Ahimsa* resolves itself into love, and love in turn resolves itself into knowledge, for action depends upon feeling, and feeling in turn depends upon understanding. *Ahimsa* is "the outward and visible sign of an inward and spiritual grace," the external expression of an internal realization. We should try to find out what that understanding, grace or realization is, for without it the practice of *ahimsa* is impossible.

To begin with, it is necessary to understand correctly in what ignorance essentially consists, for knowledge is in its negative aspect nothing but the absence or privation of ignorance. The Buddha has repeatedly affirmed that the one root-illusion which proliferates into all the miseries and misconceptions to which our mortal flesh is heir, which lies at the back of every greedy, cruel or deluded thought or word or deed, is the tightly-clung-to belief that we are individual selves or separate ego-entities which are divided by an impassable gulf of difference from all other similarly constituted selves or ego-entities whatsoever. To this view, in its most refined no less than in its grossest formulations, the Buddha gave the name of Atmavada or philosophical Egotism. He made it perfectly plain that wheresoever lurked even the subtlest sense of separative selfhood there lurked also incipient the germs of greed, cruelty and delusion, and therefore of birth, disease, old age, death and every other form of suffering too. Because men think and feel themselves to be little hard cores of separative selfhood, with interests and ambitions which differ from, or at times even directly clash with, the interests and ambitions of all the other millions of similarly constituted "selves", they naturally behave and act as such, and their behaviour and actions are naturally either centrifugal movements of attraction to the "pleasant" which we call desire (*lobha*) or centripetal movements of repulsion from the

27

"painful" which we call hatred (*dosa*). It is not difficult for a child, even, to understand that *Atmavada*, egotism, or, in plain Anglo-Saxon, selfishness, in one or another of its innumerable forms, is the root cause of all the wickedness, and therefore of all the misery, which has ever been or which ever will be in this or in any other world. When selfish interests and ambitions are thwarted they turn into hatreds which are violent in proportion to the strength of the frustrated desire; and violence is but another name for *himsa*. Only by thoroughly uprooting the minutest fibres no less than the thickest and toughest stems of the ego-sense shall we be able to check the wild growth of hatred and arrest the exuberance of the swelling buds from which runs down the world-intoxicating wine of violence. It is for this reason that the Buddha stressed the indispensable necessity of the eradication of the ego-sense in the spiritual life and laid down the doctrine of *Anatta* or *Sunyata* as the ultimate philosophical foundation of His religion.

Since ignorance (*moha*) consists primarily in the belief that one is, has, or contains some kind of permanent and peculiar element called "soul" or "self", wisdom (*prajna, bodhi*) on the contrary consists in the knowledge that one's own and all other "personalities" or "things" whatsoever are altogether empty of any such entity, and that one's mind is a stream of psychic events even as one's body is a stream of physical events. For the foolishness of the conception of a static being is thus substituted the wisdom of the realization of a dynamic Becoming. Into the genesis of the illusion of permanence it is not our intention now to enquire, but irrefragably true and certain it is that until this most pernicious of all illusions is destroyed root and branch the full and perfect practice of *ahimsa* is impossible. To try to practise non-violence while clinging desperately to the conception of a permanent individual soul or self is like trying to row a boat which is still fastened by its hawser to the shore. The cultivation of what we may term the sense of universal emptiness is the one fundamental spiritual practice which all others must subserve. Any practice which heightens one's ego-sense, howsoever holy in popular estimation it may be, is unspiritual, and any practice which attenuates it, howsoever mean and despicable outwardly it may seem, is spiritual in the truest and best sense of the term. Growth in holiness is essentially growth in emptiness. But it should not be supposed that emptiness is equivalent to the absolute death of a blank annihilation or nothingness. Certain ignorant and malicious critics of Buddhism have indeed persistently tried to misrepresent it as such, despite the unanimous emphatic declaration to the contrary of all schools of Buddhist thought. Emptiness or egolessness is equivalent to blank annihilation only to those for whom the conception of a life of egolessness is consequently unthinkable. But those who do not thus fondly cling to the illusion of selfhood, who have learned, in the terse words of *The Voice of the Silence*, to see "the voidness of the seeming full," to understand the egolessness of all this ego-seeming existence, are able to see also "the fullness of the seeming void," to realize that emptiness instead of being a mere negation pulsates with spiritual life—with that pure and perfect life which, although appearing to our dualistic consciousness as the Life of Compassion, thinks not "I am compassionate".

It would be a mistake, however, to think of emptiness and egoless compassionate activity as two distinct principles, or even as two merely accidentally related states. They are to each other as the obverse and reverse sides of a single coin, or indeed even more intimately related than that—so intimately in fact that in the end it becomes impossible to speak of a relation at all, since to do so implies that they are in a sense external to each other, like the distinguishable although inseparable sides or angles of a triangle, whereas in truth emptiness *is* active and activity *is* empty. The realization of one is therefore necessarily the realization of the other also. If one wishes to achieve the condition of compassionate activity, which is the positive expression of the rather negative and contentless term *ahimsa*, one must first of all attain to the state of emptiness or egolessness. The "problem" of *ahimsa*, or in fact any other difficulty experienced in applying ethical principles to concrete situations in daily life and exigencies of personal conduct, arises only when it is sought to attach non-violent actions in a purely external manner to an egotistic and therefore fundamentally violent consciousness. The ego can act only egotistically. It is impossible for it to act egolessly. Only emptiness can act egolessly and compassionately and therefore non-violently also. The ego-dominated intellect is totally unable to penetrate the mystery of egoless activity. Its artificial attempts to create patterns of non-violent behaviour without first of all removing the root-cause of violence are foredoomed to failure from the very beginning. The realization of emptiness is the only way to achieve egoless, compassionate and non-violent activity for the benefit of all sentient beings.

When the ego-sense is removed compassionate activities, or in negative terminology non-violent behaviour, will stream forth spontaneously from the purified inner consciousness, just as, when the boulders which blocked its passage are removed, the mighty mountain torrent rushes downward to the plain below. Problems of conduct will no more arise. "His mind becomes peaceful, so also his speech and deeds," sings the *Dhammapada*. Conduct will automatically be non-violent when the consciousness behind it is non-egotistic. Situations which seemed to present insoluble theoretical difficulties will be entered into and solved spontaneously by enlightened practice in a manner baffling the comprehension of the ego-ridden intellect. But, although these subtler activities of emptiness in its more refined phases and more delicate shades of manifestation may elude the clumsy grasp of the dualistic understanding, the general pattern of its activity is nevertheless distinctly recognizable.

The Buddha has stated clearly and categorically that one who has realized the perfection of emptiness, and therefore also the plenitude of compassionate activity, is incapable of transgressing the fundamental rules of ethical behaviour, although for such a one obedience to the moral law indeed consists not so much in the acceptance of a code imposed from without as, on the contrary, in expression of a realization flowering spontaneously from within. Although the Arahant is "beyond good and evil" he nevertheless manifests in the field of life and action in a determinate manner as an ethical, not as an unethical, being. Buddhism thus bangs the door in the face of antinomianism and sternly rejects the pseudo-liberation which claims that one who has transcended all such relative terms as good and evil is capable of acting indifferently in a manner which is moral or in a manner which is immoral according to the canons of conventional ethics. The purely transcendental activity of ineffable emptiness manifests in the world of relativity as compassion, or rather is apprehended by it as such, and *ahimsa* or non-violence is simply the negative expression of a particular phase of that manifestation. As we have already said, *ahimsa* resolves itself into compassion, and compassion in turn resolves itself into egolessness, for action depends upon feeling, and feeling in turn depends upon understanding. Only the empty and egoless, the loving and compassionate, can practise *ahimsa*. For them only the "problem" of *ahimsa* does not arise. They alone are blest. They alone are the true Bodhisattvas, the true Shravakas.

THE NATURE OF BUDDHIST TOLERANCE

Facetious question has been made whether words reveal or conceal thought more. The kernel of truth contained in this dry old husk of a jest becomes apparent when we review the efforts made by the translators of eastern philosophical and religious texts to render terms like *karma, nirvana, citta* and *dharma* each by a single equivalent word in a modern language: one may be pardoned for feeling that all their labours have succeeded in obscuring, rather than in clarifying and illuminating, the idea which the original author sought to express.

Dense as the obscurity of verbally equivalent translations is, however, it is as nothing compared with the obscurity which ensues when eastern philosophical and religious systems are described in terms of which there is not the remotest analogy, even, in the languages through which their ideas were originally conveyed. It is often said, for example, that Buddhism is a tolerant religion, and that during the two and a half millennia of its historical existence it has exhibited tolerance unparalleled by any other creed; but neither in Pali nor in Sanskrit does any word exist of which 'tolerance' might serve as even the most approximate translation. Swami Vivekananda has said that the word 'intolerance' is not found in the Sanskrit lexicons because this socio-religious phenomenon was not found in India. Apart from the fact that the statement is historically false (for intolerance undoubtedly *did* exist in ancient India, and both Buddhists and Jains had from time to time to endure its force and fury), it might with equal truth be argued that since the word 'tolerance' is not found in Indian dictionaries, the phenomenon of tolerance is unknown in Indian life. Crudities of this sort will have to be avoided if we wish to solve the problem of how it was possible for Buddhism to exhibit the characteristic of tolerance to such a marked extent when, apparently, it had no clear conception of this particular virtue, and never sought deliberately to infuse it among its votaries. But first of all we shall have to form a clear idea of the meaning of the word upon which our whole discussion revolves.

Etymologically, the transitive verb 'to tolerate' is derived from a Latin root meaning 'to bear', and it is of interest to note that this root is akin to the Greek *tlenai*, to bear or to endure, whence is derived Atlas, the name of the giant who in Hellenic mythology supports on his shoulders the pillars of the sky. As used in English literature the word means, in addition to the primary sense which it has inherited from its Latin ancestor, firstly "To suffer to be, or to be done, without prohibition or hindrance; to allow or permit negatively, by not preventing; as, to *tolerate* doubtful practices," and secondly "To bear the existence of thorough indifference or lack of interest; to put up with."* Though originally applied to disagreeable things, persons or occurrences, it was not long before the application of the word was enlarged so as to include opinions and ideas on all subjects, but particularly those connected with religious doctrines and beliefs.

The nouns 'toleration' and 'tolerance' are the results of this extension. By toleration is meant the "Act or practice of tolerating; specif., the policy, usually governmental policy, of permitting the existence of all (or given) religious opinions and modes of worship contrary to, or different from, those of the established church or belief; recognition of the right of private judgement, esp. as to religious matters," while by tolerance is meant "The act, practice or habit of tolerating; the quality of being tolerant; specif., the disposition to tolerate, or allow the existence of, beliefs, practices, or habits differing from one's own; now often, freedom from bigotry; sympathetic under-

*Webster's New International Dictionary, 2nd Edition, London, 1937.

33

standing of others' beliefs, etc."*

An examination of these definitions reveals that the object tolerated is in normal circumstances repugnant, or even positively painful, to the person by whom it is tolerated. When this object is a religious doctrine it becomes more painful still; for a belief which contradicts one's most cherished convictions is regarded not merely as an error of judgement, but as a personal affront, as a threat to the security of the state, and even as a menace to mankind. Our natural reaction to pain is aversion or, to pain inflicted by a living being, hatred; and hatred leads, sooner or later, to violence. That species of hatred which is excited by the existence of opinions, particularly religious opinions, contradictory to, or merely different from, our own, is known as intolerance; and the kind of violence which such hatred engenders is known as persecution. Since opinions originate not by themselves, but from human brains, intolerance is felt for, and persecution directed against, not merely the thoughts but the thinkers. In Christian Europe the burning of heretical books led quite naturally to the burning of the heretics themselves. Given the dogmatic premises of Roman Catholic theology, a philosophically minded historian, had such a being existed in the fourth or fifth century A.C., could probably have predicted in detail the atrocities of the wars of religion and the enormities of the Holy Inquisition a thousand years later. That the peoples of the West have become comparatively tolerant during the four or five generations which have passed since those pious days is due to the operation of two kinds of factors, one acting externally on ecclesiastical corporations, the other internally on the hearts and minds of men.

In the first kind of factor may be included historical events such as the collapse of Papal Supremacy, the disestablishment of the Russian Orthodox Church, the strict separation between Church and State which was decreed in many countries and,

*op. cit.

34

in Protestant lands, the necessity of adjusting the rival claims of a host of mutually hostile sects. All these events resulted in a drastic curtailment of the political power which had been wielded for centuries by religious bodies. They wrested the sword from the Church's bloodstained grip. Those in whose heart the fire of fanaticism burned as fiercely as ever ceased to persecute, not because they had ceased to hate those who held convictions different from their own, but simply because the power to persecute had been taken from them. The dogmatic premises of Roman Catholicism, for instance, have not changed since the palmy days when heretics were tortured in the dungeons of gloomy castles, or with civic pomp and religious ceremony burned alive at the stake in public squares. The Church is still by no means unwilling to wound, and recent events in some of the South American republics, such as Columbia, where Protestants have been burned and drowned and tortured to death, have shown that, whenever the sword of political power is restored to her hands, she is by no means afraid to strike.

In the second kind of factor which has contributed to the comparative tolerance of the modern West may be included all those scientific discoveries which have disproved the Church's dogmas, challenged the exclusive truth of its revelation, and weakened the faith of many of its supporters. The so-called tolerance of Christian lands today is, therefore, largely due to the fact that the intolerant are rarely able to exercise political power, while those who do exercise political power seldom have so much misguided zeal for their religion that they are willing to persecute on its behalf. Such tolerance as exists is, in fact, little more than the joint product of impotence and indifference. The only kind of positive factor to be noted is the steady growth of belief in the right of private judgement in religious matters, of the freedom of individual men and women to decide for themselves what their personal attitude towards the deepest things of life will be.

This third factor operates, however, upon the minds of a cultivated minority, and does not exercise any direct influence on the conduct of the majority of nominally Christian folk.

The same principle of freedom of thought was not only accepted by the Buddha, but clearly enunciated and uncompromisingly upheld by him throughout the five-and-forty years of his earthly ministry. He repudiated Vedic authority and ridiculed the pretensions of the Brahmins. In the *Kalama Sutta*, which may be described as Humanity's Charter of Religious Freedom, he advised the Kalamas of Kesaputta, whose minds had been confused by the dogmatic assertions and exclusive claims of the sectarian teachers of that period, not to go by hearsay nor to rely on tradition, nor even on inference, nor to defer out of respect to the opinions of the professionally religious. In accordance with the severely pragmatic character of his doctrine, he urged them to submit all teachings to the test of personal experience, and to reject those which were blameworthy, which were contemned by the wise, and which would, when followed out and put in practice, conduce to loss and suffering.* Still clearer and more positive were the words which the Tathagata addressed to Mahapajapati, his maternal aunt and foster-mother: "Of whatsoever teachings, Gotamid, thou canst assure thyself thus: 'These doctrines conduce to passions, not to dispassion; to bondage, not to detachment; to increase of (worldly) gains, not to decrease of them; to covetousness, not to frugality; to discontent, and not content; to company, not solitude; to sluggishness, not energy; to delight in evil, not delight in good; of such teachings thou mayest with certainty affirm, Gotamid, 'This is not the Norm (*Dharma*). This is not the Master's Message.' But of whatsoever teachings thou canst assure thyself (that they are the opposite of these things that I have told you),—of such teachings thou mayest with certainty affirm: 'This is the Norm. This is the Discipline. This

*Anguttara Nikaya I. 188.

36

is the Master's Message'."*

By living in accordance with the Dharma, by practising its successive stages of ethics (*sila*) and meditation (*samadhi*), the disciple develops an intellectual intuition (*prajna, panna*) of Reality by which he is liberated from the false conception of things as mutually exclusive ego-entities. He sees that the universe is completely empty of all separate selfhood, and that every single 'object' in fact interpenetrates, and is interpenetrated by, every other 'object'. It was this great vision of life which the Buddha sought to share with humanity, which he sent forth his Arahants to preach, and which, embodied in metal, wood and stone, depicted in line and colour, and described in rich and rhythmic verse, flooded the whole eastern world with the radiance of "a light that never was on sea or land".

To bring light means to banish darkness. When knowledge dawns, the shades of ignorance must flee away. The above quotations from the Scriptures illustrate the fact that the Buddha not only made absolutely clear what Dharma is but what it is not. With unexampled insight he analyzed the multitudinous philosophical views (*ditthi*) and religious practices (*vrata*) of his time and, by the application of the pragmatic principle, distinguished the true from the false, the right from the wrong. In the *Brahmajala Sutta*, the celebrated first discourse of the *Digha Nikaya*, he classified no less than sixty-two erroneous views, condemning them all as hindrances to the living of the holy life and the attainment of Nirvana. It should never be forgotten that, for a preacher of the Dharma, to reveal truth and to dispel falsehood are the positive and negative aspects of one process, and the history of Buddhist thought bears testimony not only to the energy with which the Message of the Master was propagated but also to the vigour with which contradictory doctrines were opposed. Buddhism has never fled to that last refuge of feeble-

*Some Sayings of the Buddha, by F.L. Woodward, pp.278-79.

minded philosophers, the vague but, apparently, consoling thought that all religions and philosophies are 'true', whatever this may be held to mean, and that they all lead, in the end, to the same destination, whatever and wherever it is believed to be. With the goal of the holy life shining clear before their eyes, and the path thereto stretching plain and straight from beneath their feet, the followers of the Buddha naturally sought to turn people aside from the false paths which led only to illusory goals.

But why was this never done forcibly and violently, with the rack and the stake, as in Christian Europe, or even with the help of an occasional outbreak of persecution, as in Hindu India or Confucian China? Buddhism was for centuries in possession of almost unlimited political influence, but not once did it invoke the aid of civil authority in dealing with its enemies. Even in lands where an ardently Buddhist monarch ruled over a devout people, the sole armour of a warrior of the Dharma was reason, his only weapon persuasion, as he endeavoured "with winning words to conquer willing hearts". For what special reason was it that the Buddhists, who believed in the truth of their religion as ardently and as uncompromisingly as any Christian bigot or Muslim fanatic, did not imitate them in the employment of political power to enforce religious conformity?

The answer to this question lies in one of the most beautiful words to be found among all the riches of Buddhist vocabulary: *Karuna*—Compassion. We have already pointed out that violence springs always from hatred, and that persecution is simply the kind of violent behaviour which results from that form of hatred we call intolerance, which is a feeling determined not only not to bear, but even to destroy, the object of its aversion. The root of hatred, as of desire, is ignorance. This ignorance is not merely intellectual, but spiritual, and consists in the erroneous conception of 'things' and 'persons' as mysteriously ensouling an unchanging principle of individuality

38

by which they are irreducibly differentiated from all other 'things' and 'persons' in the universe. The realization that concepts such as 'things' and 'persons' are in reality empty of such a principle, and exist instead in a state of "unimpeded mutual solution", destroys not only egoism but also the false views and wrong emotions which are begotten by egoism. Ignorance is transformed into wisdom, and hatred, the emotional complement of ignorance, into compassion, the affective counterpart of wisdom. False views can issue in violence, since egoism has not been destroyed, and until egoism has been destroyed ignorance and hatred will continue to spring up as luxuriantly, and spread as rapidly, as weeds do when the root has not been torn out from the ground and burned. Buddhism, since it annihilates the erroneous conception of unchanging separate selfhood, stifles as it were ignorance, lust and hatred in the womb, and permanently precludes the possibility of violence being used even for the advancement of its own tenets. The Dharma of the All-Enlightened and All-Compassionate One spares us the contradiction of spreading the gospel of love by means of the sword, and the paradox of burning alive men, women and children who entertain religious opinions different from our own, to show how tenderly we care for the salvation of their souls.

Instead, it presents us century after century with a magnificent spectacle of compassionate activity, with an ever-changing panorama or missionary enterprise whereon, as the scene shifts from country to country, and as races, cultures, religions and languages succeed each other with bewildering rapidity, there gleams unchangeably the steadfast light of love. That which shines forth to western eyes, or to eastern eyes wearing western spectacles, as the much lauded modern virtue of tolerance, is in truth what Buddhists call *upaya*, or skilful means, the radiant offspring of the embraces of *prajna* (wisdom) and *karuna* (compassion). The strength which fills the 'messenger of the Dharma' is not the restless and tumultuous energy of hate, but the placid and serene power of Love. The light which guides him on his way is not the flickering marsh-fire of dogmatic religion, which entices to betray, but the clear and steadfast radiance of Perfect Wisdom. Compassion saves him from the extreme of fanaticism, intolerance and persecution; wisdom delivers him from the opposite extreme of 'universalism' and indifference. Without compassion, he would sin against man; without wisdom he would sin against the Truth. Possessing both, he follows in the footsteps of the Supremely Wise and Boundlessly Compassionate One, treads the Middle Path and, practising the Perfection of Skilful Means, continues to pose to the modern world the problem of how a 'religion' which does not even possess a word whereby to translate 'tolerance' should yet be more 'tolerant' than many which do.

WHERE BUDDHISM BEGINS
AND WHY IT BEGINS THERE

That existence was all of a piece (whether mental or material), and that the truth about existence was therefore a whole, was, at least until fairly recent times, an article of faith more or less generally accepted among philosophers. Hence the conception of philosophy as system, as being the coherent explanation of the totality of phenomena. Hence the conception of the philosopher as system-builder, as the architect of a vast and elaborate structure wherein every fact would find its appointed place. From Plato and Aristotle to Hegel and Herbert Spencer, the ambition of philosophers has been to build ever bigger and better systems than their predecessors, just as it is the ambition of American millionaires to build bigger and better skyscrapers. Except that the philosophers have had more justification than the millionaires, for the fact-population of the philosophical world has increased enormously during the last few hundred years, and it might therefore with some plausibility be argued that extra accommodation was by this time urgently required.

If the "truth is the whole" and if philosophy is system, it follows that both are fixed and unchanging. Their universe is what William James called a block universe. Nothing ever happens in it. Nobody goes anywhere. Nobody does anything. Everything has happened and all people have gone where they wanted to go and done what they wanted to do, once and for all. Time is somehow adventitious, progress an illusion, change unreal. Existence as a whole is what it was eternally in the past and what it will be eternally in the future. We are frozen into it as a fly into a block of ice. *Sub specie aeternitatis,* everything exists simultaneously. All the philosopher has to do is to construct an exact model of existence. Hence the appropriateness of the architectural simile.

But however clear and coherent his mental blueprint may be, as soon as he commences his work of construction the philosopher is confronted by a serious difficulty. Where is he to begin? The ordinary architect is called upon to solve no such problem; whether he likes it or not he has to begin by laying the foundation. But our philosophers who build with airy concepts are not hampered by any such restraints, and may begin wherever they please, whether in the basement or the attic, down the crypt or up the steeple. Their freedom of movement is, moreover, facilitated by the fact that they are not sure in which direction "up" and "down" really are, since this would be to entertain preconceptions, and from all pre-conceptions their ideal of strict philosophical objectivity demands that they should be free; so which part of the building is the crypt and which the steeple will be known only when the structure is complete, when it stands foursquare (or whatever other shape it may be) in all its rigid perfection and immobile beauty to all the winds of change that blow. In the meantime it exists clearly and coherently enough in the mind of the architect, as we have already said, and with this fact we must be content. The only difficulty is the practical one of exposition, and merely practical difficulties have never troubled philosophers overmuch.

Reduced to its simplest terms, the difficulty in which the system-building concept of philosophy finds itself inevitably involved is that of representing serially, *as a succession of parts*, what it conceives spacially as a *simultaneity of parts*; of expressing eternity in terms of time. Since reality is not like a ball of twine, with a definite beginning and end, which can be unrolled little by little until it forms one divisible and measurable line, the difficulty is, in fact, insuperable. The eternalist view of reality pictures it as a sort of sphere or globe, and how impossible it is to make a two-dimensional pro-jection of a three-dimensional figure, all cartographers know. But books have to be written, just as maps have to be drawn, and although a philosophical work may appear to dispense with an end, it can hardly dispense with a beginning. In the absence of an objectively determinable starting-point, the system-building philosophers have therefore fallen back more or less unconsciously on their subjective preferences and made do with those.

Descartes began with *Cogito, ergo sum*, though for no better reason than that the scholastics who had preceded him began with revelation. Spinoza took as his point of departure axioms which he thought of as self-evidently true for philo-sophy as those of Euclid were then thought to be for geometry. But time, instead of confirming his opinion that there could be but one system of philosophy (whether that of Spinoza or anyone else), even as there was but one system of geometry, has on the contrary neatly controverted it with the discovery that there could be many systems of geometry, just as there are many systems of philosophy.

Hegel made a bold attempt to solve the difficulty by identifying the dialectical movement of history; but he met with no more success than his numerous predecessors. Facts stubbornly refused to be so ruthlessly conscripted into the ranks of his dialectical battalions. A crack appeared in the gi-gantic walls of his building which slowly widened until the magnificent edifice split in two, and the halves had to be dismantled and carted away for the construction of more enduring if less imposing structures elsewhere.

Since the starting point of each philosopher was different, his conclusion also was necessarily different, as well as the line of exposition by which the two were connected. Plato has conferred on the philosopher the grandiose title of "spectator of all time and all existence", but, although he tells him what to see, he does not tell him from where to see it, whether to take a bird's eye view with the transcendentalist or a worm's eye view with the empiricist.

Indian tradition considers all philosophical points of view (*darshanas*) as more or less equally valid, since Reality is ineffable, and therefore susceptible of more than one intellectual interpretation. All that is expected of any such interpretation is that it should help the person who accepts it to experience for himself the Truth which it can indicate but which it is powerless to describe. Here philosophy and religion meet. But in the West, where the intellect has generally been regarded as making a fully adequate conceptual representation of Reality, the truth of one system precludes the possibility of any other system being true. The question of any pragmatic reference did not, until the days of William James, even arise. Philosophy was one thing and religion another, and the nature of the connection between them remained a matter of uncertainty, except of course to Hegel, who crushed religion on the Procrustean bed of his dialectic as merrily as he had stretched physics. System therefore succeeded system, as century followed century, and one shaky building was put up after another so that, if today we glance backward in history, the philosophical landscape appears dotted with ruins of innumerable structures of all shapes and sizes—melancholy monuments to the pride of human intellect, which would seat knowledge in the chair of wisdom, and elevate mind to the throne of spirit.

Buddhist philosophy (and religion, for the two are inseparable and should always go together and be called *Dharma*) adopts, however, an altogether different procedure, declaring that the only possible religio-philosophical starting-point is not a thought, an idea or a concept at all, but, on the contrary, a feeling, the feeling of pain, physical and mental suffering, *dukkha*. Nor are we given a merely theoretical definition of pain, for, silently pointing to the solid and incontrovertible facts of birth, old age, disease, death, being separated from those we love, having to live with those we hate, Buddhism

44

lets them speak to us for themselves, and they whisper in the depths of our hearts the tidings that "all this is pain".

This shifting of emphasis from the cognitive to the affective modes of experience marks a change in philosophy even more radical than that brought about by the famous "Copernican revolution" of Kant, since it brings both philosophy and religion home to "men's business and bosoms" with an immediacy of impact such as no conceptual commonplace could possibly have achieved. Pain is the common ground whereon meet prince and peasant, mill-hand and millionaire, male and female, old and young, animal and vegetable, man and amoeba. Sentient existence is a great brotherhood of suffering. The same nerves that transmit sensations of pleasure can transmit sensations of pain. If it is the faith of Wordsworth that "every flower enjoys the air it breathes," it is equally the faith of the Buddhist that every blade of grass "feels with pain the sting of rain". Whether we go up or down in the scale of sentient existence, backwards or forward in time, inward into mind or outward into matter, where there is sensibility there is suffering, and without sensibility life as we know it cannot exist.

Suffering stands out in human life as clearly as the snow peaks of the Himalayas against the cloudless blue Autumn sky. Only our infatuation with transitory pleasures prevents us from seeing the fact steadily and whole. Even when we ignore the existence of pain we tacitly admit that it is there, and the more studiously we ignore it, the more damning does the admission become, until one day we are violently torn from whatever pleasure we are clinging to, and confronted with the fearful visage which we had avoided for so long. Even the conceiving of pain as "the sense of limitation" or "the feeling of finitude", useful though these variants may be for some purposes, is only too often an attempt to gloss over the uncomfortable fact of suffering. Pain is pain, the pain of a cut on the finger, of a kick on the shins, or a knife in the back or a bullet in the chest, or smoke in the eyes or mustard gas in the lungs; the pain of tooth-ache or stomach-ache; the pain of a wife's infidelity or a friend's ingratitude, of a parent's lack of understanding or a child's indifference; the pain of not getting what you want to get; of losing what you don't want to lose—all this is pain, a feeling not a concept, something to be immediately experienced, not something to be thought about. And this is where Buddhism begins. It would be impossible for it to begin anywhere else.

Although philosophers themselves may be unaware of the fact, all philosophising begins with the experience of pain, even though philosophical systems may not do so. Buddhism solves the problem of where philosophical exposition is to begin by identifying the psychological starting-point of philosophical activity itself with the logical starting-point of philosophical exposition. Philosophy and religion must begin with pain because that is where philosophising begins. In fact, it is where all the most important activities of life begin. Men philosophise for the same reason they eat and drink, make love and marry, write books, paint pictures, go on journeys, commit murder and suicide, cheat and steal, work and play— because they feel dissatisfied with their present mode of existence, their immediate experiences; and this feeling of dissatisfaction is what we call pain.

Mankind progresses for the same reason that the amoeba evolves—from irritation. There was never any flower of human achievement but some great sorrow lay at its root. The discovery of this fact, so fearfully obvious yet so flagrantly ignored, together with the recognition of all the momentous consequences which stem therefrom, was a stroke of philosophical genius of the first magnitude, and one which certainly could never have been achieved save by cognition of an altogether supernormal kind, it being the first work of nothing less than Enlightenment itself to proclaim to the world the Noble Truth of the Universality of Suffering.

Here the old charge of pessimism (a term for which there is, significantly enough, no Indian equivalent), trumped up against Buddhism ever since it became known in the West, is usually dragged in, and to the same oft-repeated question, the same almost equally oft-repeated answer must be made. "Is Buddhism pessimistic?" If, by pessimism, we mean the simple recognition that there are ugly facts and uncomfortable experiences in life, then Buddhism may with justice be described as pessimistic, and not Buddhism alone, but every religion that is not content to be a mere mythology of hopefulness, and every man and woman who is prepared frankly to admit the existence of facts which are experienced by all. But if by pessimism we mean the bleak doctrine that there is no way of mitigating the evil of life, that existence is irremediably bad, and that the next best thing to not being born is to die quickly, then Buddhism is most emphatically not pessimistic. It could be called pessimistic (though only in the first sense in which we used that term) if it stopped short at the First Noble Truth. Even then it would not be untrue, but only partially true. But, since Buddhism goes on to enunciate the Second Truth of the Cause of Suffering, the Third Truth of its Cessation, and the Fourth Truth of the Way to its Cessation, it is with the grossest injustice that it can be described as pessimistic. Problems are never solved by ignoring them. The frank recognition of a difficulty is the first step towards overcoming it. As well call a doctor a pessimist because he diagnoses the disease of a patient whom he wishes to cure as describe Buddhism as pessimistic because it recognises the existence of the suffering it intends to remove.

It is easy, though, to make the mistake that Buddhism is concerned only with the removal of suffering, and it is a mistake which certain Buddhists frequently make. Just as the particular kind of pain incidental to bodily existence is a symptom of physical ill-health, so is the wider and more inclusive pain of existence itself a sign that there is something

47

radically wrong with life as a whole. In both cases we are confronted not simply with the straightforward task of relieving pain, but also with the infinitely more difficult and complex one of readjusting the unbalanced somatic or psychological condition which is its cause, thus rendering the patient physically or spiritually healthy, hale and whole.

Suffering is important, not for its own sake, but because it is a sign that we are not living as we ought to live. Buddhism does not encourage morbid obsession with suffering as though it were the be-all and end-all of existence. What we really have to get rid of is not suffering but the imperfection which suffering warns us is there, and in the course of getting rid of imperfection and attaining perfection we may have to accept, paradoxically enough, the experience of suffering as indispensable to the achievement of final success. True it is that by the experience of pain we are compelled to enter upon the Path, and true it is that when we arrive at the Goal there will be no more pain; but if we think that following the Path means nothing more than the studious avoidance of painful experiences we are making a mistake of astronomical dimensions, and plunging headlong down the path of a spiritual selfishness so utterly diabolical that it is frightful to contemplate even the idea of it.

The essence of Buddhism consists not in the removal of suffering, which is only negative and incidental, but in the attainment of perfection, which is positive and fundamental. The Bodhisattva is not afraid of suffering. He accepts it joyfully if he thinks it will assist him to the attainment of his great goal of "Enlightenment for the sake of all sentient beings". The Christian mystic would continue to love God even though cast down into Hell, for he loves God for His own sake, not for the sake of any reward, not even for happiness (though he is not unhappy, for love is happiness). It is only the spiritual individualist, the typical Hinayanist of Buddhist tradition, who "loves" God for the sake of escaping the pains of Hell. Not for our own sakes, not even for the sake of "others", should we attain the Divine, but simply and solely for its own irresistible sake.

The fact that Buddhism takes as its starting point not a concept but a feeling, has not only a philosophical but also a religious significance. It solves at one stroke a problem of methodology and a problem of practical spiritual living. It is a well-known fact, and one to which we have alluded more than once in our writings, that the theoretical understanding of religious doctrines is one thing, the practical application and realisation of them, quite another. "Five Latin words," says Aldous Huxley, "sum up the moral history of every man and woman who has ever lived:

> *Video meliora proboque*
> *Deteriora sequor.*

(I see the better and approve it; the worse is what I pursue)."*

If in truth Man was a rational animal, as the philosophers of the eighteenth century believed he was, knowing would be indistinguishable from doing, understanding equivalent to practising. But he is, on the contrary, a desiderative animal, a creature of desires, like any other animal, except that in his case the great root feelings of love and hate (in the sense of attraction to pleasant and repulsion from painful experiences) have branched out into innumerable derivative forms called emotions.† And since it is his desires, his experience of pleasure and pain which ultimately determine his behaviour, it is only by somehow appealing to and utilising them that human behaviour can be influenced and changed. Most of all must religion, which seeks to work in human nature the most radical of all possible changes, be able not only to scratch the rational surface but also to penetrate the desiderative depths of the psyche.

Stories, Essays and Poems, p.405.

†For details of the derivation of emotions from love and hate, and of these from desire, see Bhagavan Das, *Science of the Emotions*. (Third Edn.) Chapters III(B) IV and V.

By beginning with the fact of pain Buddhism involves the whole emotional nature of man from the very onset. Recognition of the First Noble Truth comes not as a pleasant intellectual diversion but as a terrible emotional shock. The Scriptures say that one feels then like a man who suddenly realises that his turban is in flames. Only a shock of this kind is strong enough to galvanise the whole being into action. The most astonishing intellectual discovery is no more than an agreeable titillation in the region of the cerebral hemispheres. Only when a man feels strongly will he act effectively. It is for this reason above all others that Buddhism starts not with a concept but with a feeling, not with intellectual postulation but with emotional experience. Perhaps it is for this reason that the spiritual dynamism and creativeness of Buddhism have never been exhausted; it has flowered again and again through the ages, growing not weaker but stronger, not withered but more fresh and beautiful, as the years passed and the centuries flew by on silent wings. And if there is to be in this century, as it seems reasonable to surmise, a particularly glorious efflorescence of the religion of the Enlightened One, it will be made possible only by the correct and thorough understanding of where Buddhism begins, and why it begins there.

THE FLOWERING BOWL

It is one of the postulates of modern educational theory that the mother-tongue of the student—that is to say, the vehicle of communication most natural to him—should be the medium of instruction from the earliest to the latest states of his scholastic career. Nor is the application of this principle to be confined to the sphere of secular learning, since it exercises jurisdiction with equal authority over the domain of sacred learning, of what is commonly called "religion", but has in India been known from ancient times as Dharma, and that which modern Western writers, dissatisfied with the connotation of of the word religion, now prefer to term Tradition.

That "Every man should learn the Doctrine in his own language" is a precept which the Buddha not only laid down with the utmost clarity (the occasion being when some of His Brahmin disciples approached Him for permission to render His teachings into Sanskrit verses) but which He also illustrated most abundantly in practice by preaching in the vernaculars of His time. Hence the unparalleled activity of the Buddhist missionaries in making translations and hence the prodigious bulk of Buddhist sacred literature in Pali, Sanskrit, Tibetan, Chinese, Mongolian and Japanese. A bulk which, if it possesses the disadvantage of bewildering the brain of the modern scholar with its sheer interminability—wave upon wave of books rising up and deluging him from this veritable ocean of literature—has nevertheless had the compensating advantage of preventing the growth of that bibliolatrous attitude of mind which springs up only too rapidly within the more circumscribed compass of a narrower range of authoritative texts.

51

The word "language" should not, however, be understood as limited to the expression of thoughts and desires in verbal form. A perfectly legitimate extension of its meaning enables it to include not only thoughts and desires unexpressed in words, but all those systems of thought and patterns of emotion which have been built up from them, by a process of gradual elaboration, as well. It is for this reason possible to speak of music as "the language of the soul" and as "the universal language". By "language" is here meant simply a medium by which the soul's rarest intuitions and most delicate nuances of feeling, in the first place, and experiences common to all members of the human family, in the second, are able to find expression.

It is, moreover, possible for us to speak of the whole body of human culture, with its various limbs of philosophy, the sciences, the arts, education, and so on, as being the language of humanity; the single continuous expression of the human spirit in terms of space and time, as the several "parts", in fact, of the one "speech" of man's earthly utterance. The way in which men dress, the kind of houses in which they live, the make and shape of their articles of domestic use, their manners and their social customs, are all so many minor languages, so many revelations of themselves, so many signs which are, to the eye of understanding, as intelligible as a row of words on the printed page.

But what is it precisely, one may legitimately inquire, that finds expression in the culture of humanity in the same way that the thoughts and desires of individual men and women find utterance in human speech? If culture and civilization parallel the Word, what is there behind them which parallels the Idea?

Where what have aptly been termed "traditional" cultures and civilizations are concerned, the question admits of a simple and straightforward answer: Tradition itself is what finds expression, with varying degrees of clarity and vigour of

52

utterance, through all the diversity of their outward modes. Tradition means primarily that Transcendent Knowledge gained by the wise and by Them transmitted to Their disciples, and by these to their own pupils in uninterrupted "apostolic" succession; secondarily, the Doctrine in which, for the purpose of universal dissemination, that Knowledge finds more or less adequate metaphysical formulation; and, tertiarily, all those "religious" disciplines and "spiritual" practices by means of which the Doctrine is to be understood and the Knowledge realized. Traditional cultures or civilizations are those which are vehicles for Tradition—whether in its Hindu, Buddhist, Christian, Muslim or Taoist-Confucian forms — and which, through the multiplicity of the philosophies, arts, sciences, political systems and social conventions which pertain to them, communicate in due order the traditional Methods, Doctrine and Knowledge to the men and women who are born within their respective folds. In a traditional civilization, not only is it true that

An old pine-tree preaches wisdom,
And a wild bird is crying out Truth,

but even the design of a cup, or the pattern of a plate, a minor social custom no less than a major philosophical doctrine—may serve as the means whereby a man is reminded (and reminded the more often the more closely the thread of the support concerned is woven into the texture of his daily life) of that Transcendent Knowledge which is the Goal of human existence, the alone Desirable, the truly Fair.

It is for this reason that the normative life is so much easier to live in a traditional civilization than in one which is non-traditional or even anti-traditional. It may without any exaggeration be said that it would be more profitable spiritually to be a layman in the former kind of society than to be a monk or a priest in either of the latter. A Hindu peasant or a Tibetan Buddhist muleteer is often better acquainted with the Doctrine and Methods of his Tradition than is an English archdeacon or an American bishop with those of that to which they both nominally belong.

When Buddhism overflowed the boundaries of India and poured into the surrounding Asian countries it was but natural that those life-giving waters should irrigate the fields of the hearts and minds of their inhabitants through the emotional and intellectual channels already formed there by habits and customs centuries old. Just as a man who goes to live in a foreign country learns its language, so did Buddhism acquire the language of the countries to which its beneficent influence spread, and this not only in the narrow verbal sense but also in the immeasurably wider sense to which reference has already been made.

The Transcendent Knowledge, the Doctrine and the Methods of the Indian Buddhist Tradition found new and rich expression through the peculiar social institutions and distinctive aesthetic forms of China, Japan, Tibet and other lands. The soil wherefrom the great tree of Buddhism grew may have been rich or poor, the flowers which it produced, red or white or blue in colour, but the Seed from which it germinated, and the flavour of the Fruit which it ultimately bore, were always one.

The history of Buddhist art, wherein the figure of the Buddha Himself, in any one of its innumerably varied poses, occupies the central place, affords one of the most obvious and pleasing illustrations of this process. As the Buddha-image and the Buddha-icon spread slowly to the North, South and East, from the place of their origin, a gradual transformation in their bodily proportions and their dress, took place. If the images of Gandhara, with their rounded facial contours and graceful draperies, are reminiscent of the Grecian Apollo, the frescoes of Ajanta reveal a typical young Indian prince, with all the sinuous beauty of his race; while those of China convey the sense of homely mysteriousness which might belong to an ideal Taoist sage. The Buddhas of Burma and Mongolia,

54

of Ceylon and Nepal, are no less natives of the lands which they inhabit, and faithfully reflect in their tranquil faces, the features of their worshippers, thereby giving weight to Voltaire's flippant epigram that "God created man in His own image, and man returned the compliment."

Such transformations as these are sometimes of great doctrinal significance. The sedent figure of the Indian Buddha, for instance, with eyes half closed and His begging bowl in his lap, often undergoes a° curious modification when depicted on the marvellous painted "banners" (*thankas*) of Tibet. The bowl, which Indian art leaves empty, in these Tibetan paintings often contains a ball of rice or a nosegay of flowers. While the first variation on the sacred theme may simply reflect the average Tibetan's extremely concrete and practical approach to the things of his Tradition, the second seems to suggest a deepened insight into the meaning of the symbol itself which merits more than a casual reference.

The bhikshu or Buddhist monk was originally, and still is, to a certain extent, a mendicant; one who, for the sake of being able to devote every minute of his time and every ounce of his energy to the attainment of the Supreme End of human existence, renounced all worldly pursuits, including that of earning his livelihood, and depended for the satisfaction of his bodily needs solely upon what the faithful dropped into his bowl when once a day he went from door to door in quest of alms. The begging-bowl of the Buddhist monk may therefore be considered, ethically speaking, as a symbol of renunciation, although the renunciation here contemplated is, so far as it goes, outward and superficial rather than inward and profound, an observance more than an attitude of mind, and therefore pertaining rather to Method than to Knowledge. (This is not to under-estimate its value, however, as some hasty moderns might suppose, since, in the words of Lao Tze, "A journey of a thousand miles starts with a single step," and in every educational system the way to the higher grades lies inescapably through the lower ones.)

When, however, renunciation is considered as belonging not merely to the ethical, but as operative in the intellectual and spiritual orders as well,—when, that is to say, it is more deeply understood as the transcending of all dualistic concepts and separative movements of the will—then the empty begging-bowl of conventional mendicancy becomes the symbol of absolute spiritual poverty, of complete conceptual nakedness, of utter self-deprivation—in a word, of *Sunyata*, the voidness, itself.

It was perhaps due to the predominantly cognitive character of the genius of Indian Buddhism that it stressed so emphatically, particularly in its *Sunyavada* form, that Reality which transcends absolutely all the categories of our understanding, for ever towering with implacable and terrifying otherness above every conceptual limitation that we seek to impose upon it. Of this phase of Enlightenment, wherein is annihilated every vestige of ideation, the empty begging-bowl of the mendicant monk is a fitting symbol.

But when Buddhism penetrated northward across the mountain barriers of the Himalaya and began to inhale the bracing air of the lofty Tibetan plateau, a gradual shifting of emphasis occurred. The virile and energetic genius of the Tibetan people was not fully satisfied by a simply negative representation of the content of Enlightenment, and before long their innate spiritual athleticism succeeded in educing therefrom some of its more positive and dynamic elements.

The Compassion Aspect of the Buddha-Nature was emphasized and received a novel development in the doctrine of the *tulkus* or *nirmanakayas* of various Bodhisattvas, of whom Avalokitesvara, the Patron of Tibet, is the most prominent. The Tibetan yogis revelled in the experience of the Power Aspect of Enlightenment, and portrayed it in their sacred art under numberless vigorous and fearful forms. When studying the Tibetan religious genius one is struck by its consciousness

56

of and delight in the unbounded Compassion and inexhaustible Energy which stream forth from the bosom of Reality. That which appears as darkness and stillness to the eye of the conceptual understanding is to their glad vision full of sonorous light. Of this dynamic aspect of Reality, within whose apparent emptiness spring up exuberantly transcendent Wisdom, Love and Power, the flowering bowl which Tibetan art places in the hands of the Buddha is a not inappropriate symbol.

It should not be thought that such a development in any way constitutes a deviation from the Doctrines and Methods of the original Indian Tradition. What the Indian gurus transmitted to their Tibetan pupils was, fundamentally, the experience of Enlightenment, and while this element of the traditional complex remains constant and unchanged in the Tibetan as in every other branch of Buddhism, the Doctrines and Methods by which it was mediated, and which are its supports and instruments, were emphasized here and adapted there in accordance with the spiritual requirements of the Tibetan people. The Buddhism of Tibet has not planted flowers in the Buddha's bowl, but simply provided conditions suitable for the germination of seeds that were there from the beginning.

If the figure of the Buddha is understood as the symbol of Reality as it exists beyond all conceptual determinations, positive as well as negative, the Flowering Bowl (not merely, be it noted, the bowl *containing* flowers) which He holds in His hands may be regarded as the symbol of the dual determinations which we are compelled to superimpose upon It—that of the Wisdom of the Voidness and that of Compassionate Activity, which an alternative symbolism represents statically as being in a state of inseparable Union, and which our symbolism represents dynamically, the one springing up inexhaustibly in exuberant efflorescence from the other.

THE DIAMOND PATH

The doctrine that the conception of a separate soul, self or ego-entity is illusory forms, negatively speaking, the ultimate plinth and foundation of the entire vast superstructure of Buddhist philosophy and religion. Every single precept of ethical behaviour, each prescribed method of meditation and higher spiritual practice, is directed towards the eradication of that sense of separateness which seeks to build up "narrow domestic walls" between its own small individual life and the vast universal life which flows on all around it. Nothing in the material or spiritual universe exists in complete, or really even in partial, isolation from the remainder of that all-embracing whole of existence of which it is so integrally a part, and to shut one's eyes to this supremely important fact—the positive expression of the negative doctrine of Anatta or selflessness—is deliberately to deprive oneself of that insight into the mutuality and interpenetratingness of all things which is simultaneously the secret of liberating Wisdom and of redeeming Compassion.

> *Nothing in this world is single,*
> *All things, by a law divine,*
> *In one another's being mingle,*

sang the poet Shelley in a moment of inspiration. Every individual thing in the universe continually transcends the limitations of its own individuality by reflecting in the depths of its being the image of every other thing in the universe. The very content of its own 'individuality' cries out against the lie that it is alone. By the very mouth of selfhood is blabbed the secret of selflessness. It was not merely in hyperbole that the poet-seer spoke of seeing the world in a grain of sand, heaven in a wild flower, the universe in the palm of his hand, and eternity in an hour, but with all the stark literalness of real mystic experience. The highest things are reflected in the lowest, just as the lowest are in their turn reflected in the Highest. Nirvana or Buddhahood is reflected in the heart of every sentient being as the *Tathagatadhatu* or Element of Buddhahood, in the development of which to the utmost limit of its potentialities the career of the Bodhisattva essentially consists. Similarly, the ignorance and suffering of all sentient beings are mirrored in the very heart of Enlightenment, which is the philosophical explanation of why the Bodhisattva even after his 'Nirvana' continues to work for the salvation of the world. All things in the universe are, in the philosophico-poetical language of Asvaghesha, perfumed as it were with Suchness (the ontological aspect of Nirvana or Buddhahood) just as a garment is made fragrant by the intangible scent of flowers. Every single thing in the universe, however mean or insignificant it may outwardly seem, bears deep within itself as the truest and most essential part of its being the trace of absolute purity and perfection. This is the famous Jewel which the great Sanskrit mantra *Om mani padme hum*, so beloved of the people of Tibet, informs us lies hidden in what is, micro-cosmically speaking, the heart-lotus of every being, and what is, macrocosmically speaking, the world-lotus of mundane existence itself.

Thus it is possible to analyze every single object in the universe into an Absolute, Nirvanic or perfect aspect, and a relative, Samsaric and imperfect aspect. In Tantric Buddhism the former is often spoken of as the Vajra or Diamond aspect of existence. Everything possesses a Diamond or Noumenal aspect corresponding to its material or phenomenal aspect. Corres-ponding to the simple earthly flower springing up from the soil there is a transcendental Diamond Flower, which is that aspect of the flower in which it is perfumed by, or in which it reflects and is reflected by, the reality of Suchness. Similarly, as the transcendental aspect of our fickle and unsteady mundane mind there exists the mind which is "pure and hard as flaming diamond," the *Vajrachitta*—human personality in its highest possible aspect of freeness, mutuality and interpenetratingness with regard to all other things in the universe. That highest and most real aspect of existence in which everything interpenetrates every other thing, and wherein everything reflects, and is in turn reflected by, every other phenomenon (offering no obstruction to each other whatsoever, like the mutual interpenetration of innumerable beams of coloured light), is called the *Dharmadhatu*, the Realm of Truth, or the *Vajradhatu*, the Diamond World. The Bodhisattva aspires to live in this world, the world of realities, instead of in that presented by the ordinary mundane consciousness, the world of illusions. This does not mean that he tries to run away from this world to some other world supposed to be existing on the other side of the universe. The so-called objective universe exists only in relation to our own minds: it would be more correct to say that the world exists in us than we in it. Consequently, real change of place can be effected only by a radical change of mind, that is to say, by a transformation in the state of consciousness of the subject. The Bodhisattva transports himself from the realm of mundane existence to the Realm of Truth, the Diamond World, by realizing that the two worlds are in reality one world, and that all he has to do is to give up perceiving things in their illusory aspect of separate mutually exclusive realities, and to learn instead to perceive them in their Absolute or Diamond aspect as the parts of a perfectly interpenetrating Whole.

The spiritual life does not consist, as it is so often mistakenly supposed to do, in the mere denial of, or flight from, the things of the 'world' to the things of the 'spirit', as though the latter stood over-against the other or looked down upon them with a fierce scowl of irreconcilable opposition. This kind of attitude results only in repression and in all the evils which are inevitably attendant upon repression. All systems of spiritual culture which are founded upon a dualistic philosophy ultimately create a split in the psyche, with the result that the total energy of the individual is expended in the exhausting struggles which are continually taking place between the 'higher' and 'lower' aspects of personality, instead of being devoted exclusively to the realization of Nirvana. The problem of the spiritual life is essentially dynamic. It consists not in the understanding of spiritual truths, but in integrating the dissipated psychic energies of the individual for achieving the realization of these truths. The Tantric Buddhist system of spiritual culture, being founded upon a non-dualistic (though this does not mean upon a monistic) philosophy, neither creates conflict in the psyche nor dissipates its psychic energies. It teaches the devotee neither to fight with nor to fly from mundane things, but simply to view them in their Absolute or Diamond aspect. The Bodhisattva should feel that he is really all the time living in the Realm of Truth, the Diamond World, and that it is only the blindness of his ignorance which prevents him from realizing this fact. He should try to view all the important relationships and experiences of life in their noumenal aspect, feeling, even though he cannot clearly perceive, that the mundane things in the midst of which he lives and moves and has his being are simply the ghostly shadows of these bright realities which collectively make up the Diamond World of perfect mutual interpenetration. However gross the relationship, however mundane the experience, the Bodhisattva knows that the Diamond aspect of it is there all the time, and upon this he therefore seeks to direct his gaze, this he strives to develop and cultivate so that it gradually absorbs all the psychic energies which were formerly sucked in by its mundane counterpart.

The Tantric Buddhist religious discipline has not hesitated to cultivate in this way even the relationship which in its lowest form is based upon sexual desire. Instead of denouncing sexual relations as sinful and demanding the complete in-hibition of sexual feeling, it exhorts the aspirant to understand and develop the transcendental or Diamond aspect of these relations and feelings. Even in ordinary sexual desire there is often present a quality of self-sacrifice or self-abnegation which helps to sanctify it. If this aspect of the relation in question is cultivated, the creative energies usually absorbed in the gratification of desire will be liberated in the direction of self-transcendence. This is not for one moment to suggest that the Tantric Buddhist teaching in its purity encourages the physical gratification of sexual desire. It merely states the way in which that desire, and even the act of its physical gratification, can be dealt with when it happens to be present, or chances to occur, so as to make ultimately for liberation instead of for bondage. A famous Tantric Buddhist verse declares that the yogi is liberated by those very practices by which others are bound. It is important to remember, however, that such practices liberate him only to the extent that he succeeds in cultivating the element of self-transcendence which they contain, and bind him to the extent that he merely enjoys the element of self-indulgence like any ordinary mortal. A love-relation which involves sensuous gratification of any sort can carry the aspirant along only the most elementary stages of the Diamond Path. But a passion intense and pure as that of Dante for Beatrice involves such an immense concentration of psychic energy that when the phenomenal aspect of the loved person is swallowed up in the transcendental Diamond aspect, this concentration of energy is released with a velocity so tre-mendous that the whole personality of the lover is lifted up and carried far within the boundaries of the Diamond World. It will be noted that in this system of spiritual discipline love-relation with another human being, not with a mythological personage or imaginary deity, is sought to be cultivated. For in common with all other schools of Buddhism the Tantric tra-dition considers the conception of an anthropomorphic creator-god to be a delusion, and hence a source of bondage, so that no practice based upon belief in the truth of this delusion can be a source of liberation.

Another emotionally rich and important sphere of human activity and experience is the aesthetic. It has been recognized even in the West (by Schopenhauer) that all great Art contains an element of self-transcendence akin to that which constitutes the quintessence of religion. When this element of self-transcendence is consciously cultivated in poetry, in music, or in painting and sculpture, instead of the element of mere sensuous appeal, Art ceases to be a form of sensuous indulgence and becomes a kind of spiritual discipline, and the highest stages of aesthetic contemplation become spiritual experiences. This is, perhaps, the chief reason for the truly tropical iconographical richness of Tantric Buddhism. A system of spiritual culture aiming at the concentration and canalization of emotion, which is the precious life-blood equally of religion and of art, and which moreover professes to develop the transcendental aspect of every variety of human experience, can hardly fail to be applied to such a vast and legitimate sphere of its activity as that of the fine arts.

The sphere of love-relation and aesthetic experience are but two of all those exploited in the interests of the religious life by the Tantric Buddhist system of spiritual culture, a system which aims at revealing the transcendental aspect of every phenomenon of human consciousness, and which thereby seeks to disengage the psychic energies from the multiplicity of empirical objects over which they are normally dissipated and to liberate them in the direction of Enlightenment. But these two important examples are sufficient to illustrate in a general way the spiritual alchemy by which the dross of mundane experience is transmuted into the pure gold of transcendental experience and intuition. Through this alchemy the Great Work of Enlightenment is accomplished, and the Bodhisattva traverses within the depths of his own mind the Diamond Path which leads from the mundane world of separative and mutually exclusive existences to the Realm of Truth, the Diamond World, the world of the perfect mutuality and interpenetration of all things.

GETTING BEYOND THE EGO

Almost all religions have recognized, albeit with varying degrees of emphasis, that the eradication of egoism, or the illusory sense of separative selfhood, is the central and most essential task of any genuinely spiritual life. From the most primitive tribal taboos to the most highly developed systems of altruistic ethics their function is one and the same: to curb and gradually to eliminate that instinct of self-assertion which is, in gross or subtle form, the principal characteristic of all grades of sentient existence.

Some religious teachings, such as those of original Christianity and Islam, but dimly perceived, and then only in its darker shades and more tangible aspects, the mighty and mysterious workings of the peril-fraught sense of separative selfhood; while another teaching, like Buddhism in all its branches, has turned the searchlight of its enquiry onto its finest and whitest forms, mercilessly exposing its subtlest expressions and delicatest nuances.

All can recognize for what it is the coarse egoism which fights and struggles to possess material things, or the slightly less coarse egoism that craves for power, praise or fame; but to few indeed is given that piercing eagle vision which can discern the egoism lurking in the desire for eternal life, or in the longing for communion with some personal god.

In accordance with the superficiality or profundity of its understanding of the extent to which egoism dominates and controls human life, so are the prescriptions for its elimination which are given by a religious teaching more or less radical in character. Some are satisfied with the renunciation of the cruder forms of lust and hate, such as murder, theft and adultery, but tolerate and even approve the more refined forms of these same separative passions, such as the craving for immortality, or the belief in some ghostly "higher" selfhood which is supposedly more real than the "lower" kind. Buddhism, however, is satisfied with nothing less than the absolute renunciation of the ego-sense in its subtlest no less than in its grossest formulations, and with the all-compelling Mantra of *Anatta* exorcizes even the most tenuous spectre of selfhood.

But so much at least is clear: that the true spiritual aspirant, to whatever religious denomination he may belong, finds himself confronted from the very beginning with the problem of eliminating the sense of separative selfhood, and finds, moreover, that certain means, certain spiritual practices, are available to him for this purpose. He may devote himself to prayer, meditation or philanthropic works, with the hope of eliminating his selfish desires and becoming completely self-less in thought, word and deed. He may flagellate his body or fast, he may observe a vow of silence, or, like St Simeon Stylites, he may spend his life squatting on the top of a pillar. He may read the lives of saints, or give in charity to the poor, or pass many silent days and nights in exalted states of superconsciousness. And it will seem as though his ego-sense was becoming attenuated. But if we look closely into his state of consciousness we will find that without exception it takes the form of "*I* am fasting", "*I* am praying", "*I* am meditating", or even "*I* have attained". We find, in other words, that the ego-sense has not been eliminated, but that it has simply been dissociated from "worldly" activities and associated with "religious" activities. The net result is almost the same. The ego functions with full force and in fact all the more dangerously for that its presence and activity are not perceived.

Here we encounter in its acutest form the central problem

66

of the spiritual, as distinct from the merely religious, life. The ego-sense, the sense of separative selfhood, together with all those blind movements of attraction and repulsion which it inevitably involves, is to be eliminated, and certain practices are available for that purpose; but the ego-sense, instead of being eliminated thereby, simply transfers itself to those very practices which were intended to annihilate it. Like an unwanted but faithful dog, it is kicked out of the front door only to creep in at the back. Herein lies the tragedy of many a spiritual life. The more we struggle to eliminate our ego-sense the subtler and stronger and more dangerous it becomes. We revolve within a vicious circle from which there seems to be no possibility of escape. The man who thinks "I am enlightened" is equally far from Nirvana as the man who thinks "I am rich". The saint may be more attached to his sanctity than the sinner to his sin. In fact, a "good" man's core of separative selfhood is often harder and more impenetrable to the Infinite Light of Amitabha than that of a "bad" man shattered into humility and repentance by the consciousness of his sinful deeds.

What, then, is the way out of the difficulty? Certainly not by ceasing from activities, for that is impossible for beings whose very stuff is flux and change. The choice which we are called upon to make is never between action and inaction, but only between one action and another, and ultimately between egoistic and non-egoistic or empty actions. But what actions are non-egoistic or empty? Are there such actions, and how are we to recognize them? We have already seen that any action, however holy or altruistic it may outwardly seem, may be smirched and tainted by the sense of separative selfhood. The very radicalness of the difficulty provides the key to its own solution. We are not to imagine that we have to look for any separate class or kind of non-egoistic activities, for the fact that the ego-sense may attach itself to any action has already precluded that possibility; but we have simply to change our

67

attitude towards our action. We have to act without the sense of "I" or "mine". This is not nearly so easy as it sounds. The problem of inaction (which is what non-egoistic action amounts to karmically) has to be solved in the very midst of action. Activity must stream forth from the very heart of emptiness.

But by what practical method or by what spiritual discipline are we to eliminate that sense of "I"-ness which seems to cling fast to everything we do, dragging it down into the mire of selfhood and besmirching even the skirts of sanctity? The question tacitly reverts to that very attitude which is productive of the problem of non-egoistic action. We do not have to take up any method or discipline, we do not have to perform any new action, but simply to change our attitude to what we are already doing, to act without the egoistic consciousness of acting.

The non-egoistic attitude assumes two principal forms. In the first, all activities are attributed to The Other, and the subject confesses his utter inability to perform any action whatsoever, whether good or bad. This is the devotional form of the non-egoistic attitude. Herein the devotee surrenders himself body and soul to the object of his adoration. In the second form of the non-egoistic attitude the practitioner simply watches himself as he performs the various actions of life, whether sacred or profane, and constantly bears in mind that they are all egoless and empty, that there is action but no actor, deed but no doer. This is the more intellectual form of the non-egoistic attitude. By these two methods the ego-sense is gradually attenuated. But although the first or devotional form of the non-egoistic attitude is able to eliminate the grosser kinds of egoism it is not able to eliminate the subtler kinds, for the subject stands irreducibly over-against The Object to the very end, and it is therefore necessary to have recourse to the second or more intellectual method if the elimination of the ego-sense is to be complete.

68

Moreover, the idea of The Other is usually that of a more or less anthropomorphic deity, usually credited with the creation of the world, and to whom only good qualities are generally attributed. This raises several theological difficulties, such as the origin of evil, and since the devotee naturally shrinks from attributing his sinful actions to the deity his renunciation of his actions cannot be carried to its logical extreme, and he is compelled to confess that the sinful actions at least are his own. Consequently, recourse to the other form of the non-egoistic attitude, wherein no such difficulties arise, is sooner or later inevitable. The sense of all-pervading emptiness is the only key to non-egoistic action.

When this point is arrived at the practitioner realizes that it is not necessary to perform any "religious" action, but that those actions are in the deepest and truest sense religious wherein is no sense of agency, no feeling that "I am the doer". It should not be supposed, however, that this doctrine countenances any form of antinomianism. We have said elsewhere that although emptiness or egolessness transcends the purely empirical distinction between moral good and evil it nevertheless expresses itself in the field of life and action in a determinate manner as a moral, not as an immoral, activity, and that the very essence of this activity is compassion. It is impossible that a man who is fully enlightened, that is to say, who is absolutely empty of selfhood, should be able, as some sects teach, to kill or to steal, to commit the sexual act or to tell lies. Those who assert that the trans-moral superman or "living-free" (jivan-mukta) may act indifferently either in a moral or an immoral manner are simply fashioning a philosophical cloak for their own ethical nakedness. The activity of emptiness is ever serene and harmonious, and appears in the world as a beneficial force fighting on the side of the good for the ultimate triumph of truth and righteousness. That is why the Jewel of Transcendental Wisdom, the *Vajracchedika Prajnaparamita Sutra*, says that the

Bodhisattva engages himself in the salvation of all sentient beings at the same time that he realises that there are no sentient beings for him to save. The spiritual life is in the highest sense purposeless.

Although the criterion of the spirituality of any action consists in the presence or absence of ego-sense, there is a class of actions which are inseparably connected with the ego-sense, or which are simply the outward forms or expressions of that sense, and which it would be a contradiction in terms to speak of as being performed egolessly. With the exception of this class of actions (to which belong killing, stealing, unchastity and falsehood), every one of which is to be completely eschewed, all actions are to be performed with full mindfulness of their essentially empty and egoless nature. As this sense of universal emptiness and egolessness gradually deepens it will begin to vibrate, as it were, and flashes of compassion will dart forth with greater and greater frequency. Beneficial activities for the sake of all sentient beings will spontaneously manifest themselves. But these compassionate activities, also, the practitioner will perceive to be absolutely empty of all selfhood. Even while engaged in the lofty task of universal salvation he will not cherish the illusory idea that he does, nor that there are beings to whom he does, anything at all. The more vivid and intense becomes his realization of emptiness, the more abundant become his compassionate activities for the sake of all sentient beings. Again, the more abundant become his compassionate activities for the sake of all sentient beings, the more vivid and intense becomes his realization of emptiness. In this way the follower of the Buddha solves in his own life the problem of egoless activity.

Those who perform even "good" actions with the egoistic consciousness of doing good, who appropriate the "goodness" of an action to themselves, clinging to it and seeking to use it as a badge wherewith to distinguish themselves from others less obviously virtuous, are bound by their "virtue" to the wheel of birth and death. The more "good" they do the more tightly they bind themselves and the more they suffer. He only is able to solve the problem of egoless action who constantly remembers that all actions are pure and void of all separative selfhood. He only is able to destroy egoism root and branch who does not claim even the most virtuous action for his "own". Such a one alone is able to remain "inactive" in the midst of action, and to realize that Emptiness-Compassion which is Buddhahood in the midst of this illusory and fleeting world.

THE WAY OF EMPTINESS

The most conspicuous thing about life is that it never remains the same for two consecutive moments; but this lack of persistent identity is a fact to which most people appear perfectly oblivious, if we judge them by their outward behaviour at least.

To the pure mind everything appears as in fact it really is: a process of unceasing flux wherein one thing continually passes over into another, and wherein all things exist in a state of "unimpeded mutual solution". In such a state of perfect mutuality there are no lines of demarcation between one individual existence and another: nothing offers any resistance to being penetrated by every other thing; but one individual existence slides smoothly and easily, as it were, into another, each into all, all into each, and all into all, like the unimpeded interpenetration of innumerable beams of light.

The pure mind perceives the world as the Pure Land, the Abode of Bliss (*sukhavati*), the Realm of Truth (*dharmaloka*), as the Buddha-field (*buddhakshetra*).

But the mind which is sullied by ignorance and desire strives to arrest the flow, to dam the river of becoming with solid blocks of concepts, to freeze the waves of change into static identities. For the characteristic of ignorance is to perceive things as different, as mutually exclusive, as things-in-themselves; while the characteristic of desire is to grasp one thing and reject another, to seek pleasure and avoid pain, to love self and hate not-self.

The impure mind perceives the world as a World of Desire (*kamaloka*) and therefore as a World of Suffering (*sahaloka*). For it is one of the paradoxes of life that none is so certain to

72

experience unhappiness as he who struggles to avoid it.

When the goal of the spiritual life is reached things are seen as they really are, although it should not be supposed that there are two worlds, one of appearance, the other of reality: the two worlds are one world. The means by which the goal is attained is the eradication of ignorance and desire. The spiritual life is nothing but a progressive loosening of the bonds of separative individuality, of selfhood and egoity. Then the universe no longer appears as an unchanging system of static things and rigid relations, but as a delightfully free and fluid interplay of constantly changing terms. It is not so much that reality changes as that reality *is* change. Spiritual life begins with one's first awakening to this fact.

The individual self is a centre from which lines of discrimination radiate in all directions. It is the innermost citadel of separateness. Only when this centre expands to infinity, only when the walls of this citadel are razed to the ground, is the consummation of the spiritual life achieved.

Liberation is not so much of the self as from the self. He who conceives the spiritual life as a means of attaining eternal bliss has not understood. The whole conception of attainment is fundamentally wrong. One has simply to break down the barriers of his separative individuality and allow himself to be penetrated by everything that exists. Then he will himself penetrate everything. This mutual penetration is liberation, is happiness.

The self is the sole obstacle to the 'attainment' of happiness. Misery is the inseparable shadow of self. And the more solid the substance is, the blacker will its shadow be. To seek happiness is to seek sorrow.

It is another of the paradoxes of life that he only is happy who does not care for happiness.

The spiritual life has no goal. The means is the goal. We do not have to attain anything, but to realize that we have already attained.

To discriminate between the goal and the means, purity and impurity, enlightenment and non-enlightenment, the Buddha and the debauchee, *Nirvana* and *Samsara*, is the work of ignorance. To want to become a Buddha is the surest way of remaining an ordinary man. One may become full of wisdom and charity and may even be able to work miracles, but he will not be a Buddha. To aspire to *Nirvana* simply strengthens the bonds of desire which bind one to *Samsara*. For since these terms are all discriminated by ignorance the activities which are based upon them all take place within ignorance and do not succeed in transcending it. The more we strive to be spiritual the more unspiritual we become. The so-called religious life is fundamentally irreligious.

Even if it were possible to 'attain' Buddhahood we should still remain in bondage. For the spiritual life does not consist in the addition of any thing to the ego, however great, however spiritual, that thing may be, but in the subtraction of the ego from all things. Better to pick up a straw from the ground without a sense of ego than to attain Buddhahood with the sense of ego.

Should we, then, abandon our efforts to lead the spiritual life and attain *Nirvana*? Should we allow ourselves to slip back into the mire of *Samsara* from which we had so painfully raised ourselves a few inches? No, we should double and treble our efforts; but we should remember that all our efforts are void. We should vow to liberate all beings, to serve all Buddhas, to realize all truths, to eradicate all passions; but we should remember that in reality there are no beings to be liberated, no Buddhas to serve, no truths to realize, no passions to eradicate. To the extent that we realize their essential voidness our spiritual practices will liberate us, while to the extent that we do not realize it they will bind us.

Constant mindfulness of emptiness is the secret of success in the spiritual life. Only we must be careful not to discriminate emptiness from non-emptiness, since then it would not be emptiness but some kind of self-existence. True emptiness is empty even of the conception of emptiness. The void is itself void. Otherwise we fall into the heresy of nothingness.

Strangely enough, the remembrance of emptiness, far from decreasing one's power of spiritual activity, increases it enormously. It becomes easy, effortless, spontaneous, full of joy. Because the obstacle to activity, which is the self, has been removed.

The activity of the self is really not activity at all, and is always frustrated. The activity of emptiness is true activity, and is never frustrated.

The activity of emptiness is compassion.

Emptiness, activity and compassion are not three things, but one thing looked at from three different points of view. Where one is present, the others will be present too.

He only can feel compassion for men who realizes that there are no men for whom to feel compassion. He only can serve who is free from the thought 'I serve'.

The remembrance of emptiness is fundamental.

The fool who rushes about trying to help the world without remembering that both he and it are void simply makes confusion worse confounded and tightens his own bonds. He who sits idle thinking that the conception of emptiness exempts him from activity and excuses the hardness of his heart that does not feel compassion falls into the heresy of nothingness and is doubly lost.

But he whose activities are boundless, whose compassion is infinite, and whose remembrance of emptiness is constant and unfailing, treads the Bodhisattva-path and nears *Nirvana*.

TIBETAN PILGRIMS

From the dazzling white wastes of the Tibetan plateau, down through the steep and dangerous mountain passes, along the hot and dusty roads of what was once the Middle Kingdom, with sticks in their hands and sturdy backs bowed beneath the weight of heavy loads carried in wicker cradles, suspended from their shoulders, with the sacred mantram *Om Mani Padme Hum* ever on their lips, in rough red homespun garments, knowing no other language than their own native Tibetan, by day and by night, year after year, impelled by their simple but profound faith, come these strange pilgrims from the far-off Land of Snows. *We* have come here with all the comforts and conveniences of a second class railway carriage; but *they* have walked every single mile of the long road which stretches from their own country almost half-way across India here to Buddha Gaya. *We* admire the architecture of the Temple, speculate upon the probable date of its construction, and lament its present neglected and ruinous condition; but *their* simple faith pierces the diaphanous veil of such archaeological irrelevancies and is lost in the contemplation of the naked fact of the Lord's Enlightenment. Probably they are quite ignorant of the precise number of centuries which have passed by since He attained the sublime Consummation of His Noble Quest, and perhaps, were they questioned about it, they would scratch their touselled heads in surprise at the question and smilingly reply that they had never given thought to the matter; but from the evident earnestness with which they perform their devotions, from the unsophisticated sincerity of their demeanour, it seems as though that Great Event was as vivid and tangible to them as if the Lord had sat but yesterday upon the Diamond Throne and listened to the leaves of the Bodhi Tree whispering jubilantly above His head.

Some of the pilgrims are old, some young. Mostly they come in parties of four or five; but sometimes they arrive in pairs or singly. Some are dressed in garments of coarse red home-spun cloth, with wide swinging skirts and full bosoms, and have ornaments of silver and turquoise round their necks and suspended from holes pierced in their ears; while others are clad in filthy black tatters that flutter and dance in the breeze, and wear strings of plain wooden beads. Some are shod with scarlet or yellow Chinese boots with upturned toes, while others—the poorer sort—go barefoot. Some are heavy laden with blankets, bags of rice, cooking utensils and even little yellow-faced, rose-cheeked babies, suspended in wicker frames from their sturdy shoulders; and some carry miniature shrines of chased silver, through the tiny glass window of which is visible the gilded image of their tutelary Buddha or Bodhisattva within. A few of them carry long knives in ornamental silver scabbards slung at their side, and most of them have prayer-wheels, either tucked away idle in the capacious bosom of their dress, or twirling busily in their hand as they trudge along. But all of them, men, women and children alike, are strong-ly and sturdily built, with round, smiling, rose-cheeked faces, cheerful salutations uttered in unfamiliar speech but with unmistakable friendliness, and hearts undaunted by the diffi-culties and dangers of their long and toilsome journey. They have walked perhaps a thousand miles, enduring with equal fortitude icy snow and burning sun; they have plodded on through wind and rain and dust, beholding now the dazzling white peaks of their native Himalayan ranges, now the swift-rushing streams and dense green foliage of the foothills, now the emerald rice-fields, barren burning plains and dried up river beds of India; and now at last they have reached their destination, and with broad smiles of greeting come stumbling

77

through the gates of the Rest House. They have endured great hardships and many tribulations, experiencing not only the inclemency of nature but the cruelty and heartlessness of man; for some, taking advantage of the innocence and helplessness of these travellers in a strange land, have robbed and cheated them upon the way. Yet they do not complain; nor, now that they have at last arrived, do they look for compensating comforts, but spread their blankets on the cold stone floor of the verandah, or even bivouac out in the open air.

The clear blue winter sky and hard bright sunshine are perhaps even pleasant to them in comparison with the whirling snowstorms and icy cutting winds of their native land. Before an hour has passed they have kindled a fire and cooked thereon a frugal meal of rice-gruel flavoured with bits of chopped radish, onion and chilli. Then they sit in democratic circle round their improvized kitchen and fill and refill their bowls with the steaming pottage that bubbles over the fire. They are easily satisfied, these simple pilgrim folk. They do not care for succulent dishes, nor rich clothes, nor yet for any of the luxuries which have become necessities to the pampered and perverted sons and daughters of modern city-bred civilization. Their food and clothing are simple but serviceable, even as their physical bodies are strong and sturdy, and their faith plain and unsophisticated. A casual glance might dismiss them with mingled contempt and disgust as simply ignorant and dirty. And it is indeed true that their clothes are black with grime, their hair as uncombed and thickly matted as the mane of a wild horse, and that they would perhaps have difficulty in remembering the date on which their skins last felt the contact of water. Neither are they educated in the sense in which we pride ourselves we are. Yet they carry in the bosom of their ragged, dirty garments a precious jewel which we, the doubt-torn, world-weary children of the twentieth century, would give much to possess—the precious jewel of faith.

True it is, indeed, that faith without knowledge breeds the

rank and luxuriant growth of superstition, even as it is equally true that knowledge without faith conjures up the dismal spectres of doubt and scepticism. Yet it is perhaps less difficult for faith to give birth to knowledge than it is for knowledge to generate faith. Therefore we may well envy these simple people the possession of a faith which has enabled them to scale mountains and cross deserts, to suffer patiently and cheerfully for many months' hardships which we could scarcely brook even for a single day. *Our* knowledge is a listless and anaemic thing: it does not inspire to great deeds of heroism and selfless love. But *their* faith is full of nerve and vigour: it kindles a warm and life-giving flame in their hearts, and with its beams illuminates their steps—even when they walk in a strange land. Therefore we may well wish that our complicated modern knowledge could be wedded to the simple faith of these Tibetan pilgrims—*prajna* (wisdom) united to *karuna* (compassion)—that from their mystic union in our hearts might spring forth the glorious Bodhisattva of Buddha-ward aspiration.

Some of us might even wish that we could exchange our indigent and sterile knowledge for their rich and fruitful faith. But that may never be. We are the offspring of the twentieth century, they of the Ages of Faith—yet of a faith, surely, that is not blind, but founded on a deeper, truer knowledge belonging to the race, to the civilization, ultimately to the religion they profess itself, rather than to the individual believer. But we, for all our vaunted 'knowledge', grope and stumble in the dark; while they, for all their 'ignorance', walk along the road of life with humbly bowed but unwearied bodies, and slow but steady steps—walk as though the path beneath their feet and the destination at which they would one day arrive were both plainly visible before their eyes.

O, let us doff the glittering brocade of superficial modern intelligence, and don the coarse red home-spun garment of simple faith! With the burden of long-suffering on our backs, and with the staff of endurance in our hands, let us join these

79

humble pilgrims from the mysterious Land of Snows and trudge with them along the long and dusty road that leads to Buddha Gaya. With the Sacred Words on our lips, with the golden flame of faith and love burning in the transparent alabaster chalice of wisdom within our hearts, and with the Blessed One Himself for our guide, let us set forth as pilgrims upon the Middle Way that will lead us, one day, even to the Heart's Enlightenment.